Evan Handler, Marcia Jean Kurtz, Bob Dishy, and Florence Stanley in a scene from the Manhattan Theatre Club production of *What's Wrong with This Picture?*

WHAT'S WRONG WITH THIS PICTURE?

BY
DONALD MARGULIES

★

★

DRAMATISTS
PLAY SERVICE
INC.

SPECIAL NOTE

Anyone receiving permission to produce WHAT'S WRONG WITH THIS PICTURE? is required to give credit to the Author as sole and exclusive Author of the Play on the title page of all programs distributed in connection with performances of the Play and in all instances in which the title of the Play appears for purposes of advertising, publicizing or otherwise exploiting the Play and/or a production thereof. The name of the Author must appear on a separate line, in which no other name appears, immediately beneath the title and in size of type equal to 50% of the size of the largest, most prominent letter used for the title of the Play. No person, firm or entity may receive credit larger or more prominent than that accorded the Author. The following acknowledgments must appear on the title page in all programs distributed in connection with performances of the Play:

Originally produced by the Manhattan Theatre Club on January 29, 1985.

Subsequently produced by the Back Alley Theatre in January 1988.

Originally produced Off-Broadway by the Jewish Repertory Theatre.

Originally produced on Broadway by
David Stone, The Booking Office, Albert Nocciolino, Betsy Dollinger
in association with Ted Snowdon.

SPECIAL NOTE ON SONGS AND RECORDINGS

For performances of copyrighted songs, arrangements or recordings mentioned in this Play, the permission of the copyright owner(s) must be obtained. Other songs, arrangements or recordings may be substituted provided permission from the copyright owner(s) of such songs, arrangements or recordings is obtained; or songs, arrangements or recordings in the public domain may be substituted.

"In this our life there are no beginnings but only
departures entitled beginnings ... "

Delmore Schwartz
The World is a Wedding

"Hello, I must be going."

Groucho Marx

WHAT'S WRONG WITH THIS PICTURE? was first presented in New York City by the Manhattan Theatre Club (Lynne Meadow, Artistic Director; Barry Grove, Managing Director) in January 1985. It was directed by Claudia Weill; the set design was by Adrianne Lobel; the lighting design was by Beverly Emmons; and the costume design was by Rita Ryack. The cast was as follows:

MORT	Bob Dishy
ARTIE	Evan Handler
SHIRLEY	Madeline Kahn
CEIL	Marcia Jean Kurtz
SID	Salem Ludwig
BELLA	Florence Stanley

The play had its West Coast premiere at the Back Alley Theatre (Laura Zucker and Allan Miller, Producing Directors) in Van Nuys, California, in January 1988. It was directed by Stuart Damon; the set design was by Don Gruber; the lighting design was by Larry Oberman; and the costume design was by Bob Miller. The cast was as follows:

MORT	Allan Miller
ARTIE	James Stern
SHIRLEY	Phoebe Dorin
CEIL	Patti Deutsch
SID	Sandy Kenyon
BELLA	Lillian Adams

The play premiered Off-Broadway at the Jewish Repertory Theatre (Ran Avni, Artistic Director) in June 1990. It was directed by Larry Arrick; the set design was by Ray Recht; the lighting design was by Brian Nason; and the costume design was by Jeffrey Ullman. The cast was as follows:

MORT .... Michael Lombard
ARTIE .... Stephen Mailer
SHIRLEY .... Lauren Klein
CEIL .... Barbara Spiegel
SID .... Salem Ludwig
BELLA .... Dolores Sutton

The play was produced on Broadway at the Brooks Atkinson Theatre by David Stone, the Booking Office, Albert Nocciolino and Betsy Dollinger in association with Ted Snowdon in December 1994. It was directed by Joe Mantello; the set design was by Derek McLane; the lighting design was by Brian MacDevitt; the costume design was by Ann Roth; and the sound design was by Guy Sherman/Aural Fixation. The cast was as follows:

MORT .... Alan Rosenberg
ARTIE .... David Moscow
SHIRLEY .... Faith Prince
CEIL .... Marcell Rosenblatt
SID .... Jerry Stiller
BELLA .... Florence Stanley

CHARACTERS

ARTIE, 17
MORT, 40s, his father
BELLA, 70s, Mort's mother
SID, 70s, Mort's father
CEIL, 40s, Mort's sister
SHIRLEY, 40s, Artie's mother, Mort's wife

PLACE

A middle-class apartment in Brooklyn, New York.

TIME

Some years ago.

WHAT'S WRONG WITH THIS PICTURE?

ACT ONE

At rise: a middle-class apartment in Brooklyn where shiva has taken place. As is the tradition in Jewish houses of mourning, mirrors are covered and the mourners — in this case, Artie and his father, Mort — are unshaven and in their stocking feet. Condolence cards, week-old flowers, and donation certificates are scattered about, as are paper cups, plates and platters of food; it looks as if a party has taken place — except for a memorial candle that has nearly burned out. The living room is cluttered with furniture: an older set (sofa, armchairs, lamps, etc.) and a newly delivered set, still wrapped in paper and plastic, of an entirely different style. Sid, his head bobbing back and forth, is dozing in a chair. Mort sits, despondently, on a cardboard shiva box looking at a Polaroid snapshot. His mother, Bella, is standing at the open door, saying goodbye to unseen visitors. Artie is juggling bagels.

BELLA. *(To unseen people.)* Drive carefully! Wait, Artie wants to say goodbye.
ARTIE. No, I don't ... *(She drags him to the door; he resists.)*
BELLA. Say goodbye.
ARTIE. No ...
BELLA. *(Prodding him with gritted teeth.)* Say goodbye.
ARTIE. *(Too brightly:)* Goodbye!
BELLA. *(To unseen people.)* You remembered the rugelach?

7

ARTIE. How could they forget?

BELLA. *(To unseen people.)* My pleasure. Go, go catch your elevator. We should have only *nachas*. Go, goodbye already. *(Closes the door.)* Isn't that nice? Blanche and Al? They came back after the funeral, they didn't have to pay another call.

ARTIE. They're shiva ghouls. All they *do* is go from shiva call to shiva call. They haven't paid for a meal in years.

BELLA. Is that nice? They mean well. *(She rubs a burned spot on the coffee table.)* Al's cigar I can live without. *(Ceil enters from the kitchen.)*

CEIL. Ma, you didn't have to give them the rugelach.

BELLA. What's wrong with giving them the rugelach?

CEIL. It's Morty and Artie's rugelach.

ARTIE. It's my rugelach.

BELLA. What are they gonna do with all that rugelach? It'll go bad.

CEIL. So?

ARTIE. My mother would've wanted us to have all the rugelach we wanted. *(Fakes breaking down; he laughs; a beat.)*

BELLA. Very funny. Look at your father. Look how miserable he is. Why can't you be like your father?

MORT. What?

BELLA. Nothing, darling. Shiva's over now, dear. Blanche and Al left. The last to go. They were so torn up about Shirley, I gave them a little something to take home.

ARTIE. Our rugelach. *(Ceil, on her way to the kitchen with food, bangs her leg on a piece of furniture and winces.)*

BELLA. What did you do?

CEIL. I banged my leg, Morty, that's how crowded.

BELLA. This is normal?

CEIL. I'm black and blue.

BELLA. Your sister banged her leg.

CEIL. You want to see? *(She exits to the kitchen.)*

BELLA. This is not normal.

ARTIE. You shouldn't've let them deliver this stuff, there's no room to walk.

BELLA. Blanche looks at me like what's going on here, what do I say?

ARTIE. *(Over "what do I say?")* Either we send back the new stuff

8

or we get rid of the old stuff.

MORT. No!

ARTIE. Dad, you can't hold on to everything.

BELLA. Morty, Shirley may she rest in peace, I'm sure she didn't want you bumping into things.

MORT. The stuff stays.

ARTIE. Then let's move all the old stuff into the hall. Come on, you and me.

MORT. What the hell you trying to do, Artie?! This is your mother's furniture! She sat in this sofa your mother, Artie, we watched TV here.

ARTIE. You've got to make up your mind. You can't keep all the furniture.

BELLA. You're not thinking straight, Morty, you need a vacation.

CEIL. Ma, I gotta drop you and Pop off ...

MORT. Shirley couldn't wait to redecorate.

CEIL. ... I gotta go home, feed the girls ...

MORT. She ordered this stuff months ago.

CEIL. ... and I gotta change. *(She returns to the kitchen.)*

MORT. What was I supposed to do, tell them, "No, I don't want it"?

ARTIE. Great. So we've got all this furniture but there's no room for people.

MORT. That's right! This is the way I want it, so shut your mouth! *(A beat.)* Did you look for that laundry ticket I asked you to look for?

BELLA. Look for it, darling, he's out of clean shirts.

ARTIE. *(Still on the furniture; a new idea:)* Dad, I'll call Macy's, tell them to pick it up ...

MORT. Don't you dare.

BELLA. Artie, darling, look for that ticket. Your father says your mother may she rest in peace took a whole batch to the laundry, they should've been ready *days* ago. What's your father gonna do?

MORT. I have no wife ...

ARTIE. I'm sure if we told them what happened ...

MORT. ... I have no shirts ...

BELLA. You don't know, darling. Be a good boy, look in the closet. Maybe her pockets.

ARTIE. People lose laundry tickets all the time.

9

BELLA. *(A beat.)* I'm not leaving till we find that ticket. *(Artie eagerly clambers over the sofa to get to the hall closet where he begins rummaging through coat pockets; Ceil returns from the kitchen.)*

CEIL. Morty, where did Shirley may she rest in peace keep her Tupperware? *(Mort shrugs.)*

ARTIE. In the cabinet under the sink. I'll get it.

CEIL. Never mind. Stay. *(Exits to the kitchen. Pause.)*

BELLA. Morty, you need to go away. Forget a little.

CEIL. *(Off.)* Ma ...

BELLA. I'm telling you, Morty: A change of scenery. They have trips for singles.

CEIL. *(Off.)* Ma, Morty's not interested.

BELLA. Hawaii, Mort.

MORT. Hawaii!

BELLA. You and Shirley may she rest in peace, you always talked about going to Hawaii.

MORT. I never took her to Hawaii. *Next* year, always *next* year ...

BELLA. So, go! Life is short. If you want to do, do! What are you waiting for? *(Ceil returns for more platters of food.)*

CEIL. Ma, when Morty wants to do, he'll do.

BELLA. There's a whole world out there! Europe, Mort! Africa!

CEIL. Ma, do me a favor, please, wake up Pop, I gotta get going. *(Exits to kitchen.)*

BELLA. Go to Israel. See how our trees are doing.

ARTIE. Grandma, you missed your calling. You should've been a travel agent.

BELLA. Artie, you too.

ARTIE. What.

BELLA. Go away. Sightsee. Take a day trip. Go away with your friend. That girl. The one you were with the night your mother —

CEIL. *(Off.)* Ma!

BELLA. *(A beat.)* Any luck, Artie? *(Meaning in his search for the ticket.)*

ARTIE. *(Misconstruing her question; panic-stricken.)* What do you mean?

BELLA. You find the ticket?

ARTIE. Oh. No. No ticket. Thought maybe I'd find surprise messages or secret bankbooks. Here's a tissue. *(Mort looks up.)*

She pressed her mouth to this.

MORT. Let me see. *(Artie gives it to him.)*

ARTIE. Hold on to that. It's a relic. *(Resumes rummaging.)* A couple of pennies ... an M&M. Orange. *(He eats it.)* A petrified gob of Juicy Fruit. Hold on to that, too, Dad. *(Hands it to Mort, continues.)* Lots of lint. Big on lint. *(Finds a matchbook, reads it.)* Oh, and a matchbook. Dad, when were you and Mommy at the Holiday Inn in Freehold, New Jersey?

MORT. No, the Poconos. I took her to the Poconos.

ARTIE. Ever stop over in Freehold?

MORT. Freehold? That's where bosses take their secretaries for a lunch hour shtup. No, your mother was a real lady. I took her to the Poconos. We watched dirty movies in a heart-shaped tub. *(Artie pockets the matchbook.)*

BELLA. You're out of shirts, too, Artie?

ARTIE. I have shirts.

CEIL. Ma ...

BELLA. T-shirts at shiva?

CEIL. Leave him.

BELLA. I'm not saying a *tie* ...

CEIL. *(Exiting.)* It's his way.

BELLA. *(To Artie.)* What would your mother say?

ARTIE. Right now not much.

BELLA. *(Perturbed; changes the subject.)* Morty, what are we gonna do about your shirts?

ARTIE. Why don't you go home, if I find the ticket, I'll call you.

BELLA. What, you don't need me anymore? You don't need anybody? You're all grown up? Wait. *(Ceil returns.)*

CEIL. Ma, I told you to wake up Pop. God, Ma! *(Exits. Artie goes to Sid, gently shakes him.)*

ARTIE. Pop? Pop? *(Sid stirs, awakens.)*

SID. Bella? *(Artie points to Bella.)*

BELLA. I'm here, Sid.

SID. Bella, I was stuck in traffic on the Williamsburg Bridge. A couple of guys tried washing my windshield but my windshield wasn't dirty.

BELLA. You want something, Sid?

ARTIE. Pop, let me get you a drink. *(He starts for the kitchen.)*

11

SID. Uncarbonated.

ARTIE. I know. *(Exits. Mort is lost in reverie over the tissue.)*

BELLA. *(To Mort.)* Ever since The Heart Attack, he hasn't had a drop of soda.

SID. Soda makes me greps. Every time I gave a greps, I thought I was having a heart attack. *(Artie returns, hands Sid a glass of water.)* Thanks, son. No bubbles? *(Artie nods; Sid sips the water.)* Okay.

ARTIE. I'm glad, Pop. You're tired, hm? *(Sid shrugs.)* Grandma, Pop's tired. You should take him home.

BELLA. He's always tired. Nothing new.

MORT. *(Obsessing aloud.)* I wanted to go to the deli. No, she had to try this new Chinese restaurant.

BELLA. Morty's at it again, Ceil. *(Sid, also fed up with Mort's tirade, exits to the kitchen; Bella flips through a magazine.)*

MORT. That was Shirley ...

CEIL. *(Off.)* Ma, let him talk it out.

MORT. ... always trying new things.

CEIL. *(Off.)* He's got to get it out of his system.

MORT. We stood in line twenty minutes so Shirley could choke to death on a thing called "moo shu pork."

BELLA. Again with the moo shu! *(Sid returns from the kitchen eating a plum.)*

SID. Artie?

ARTIE. Yeah, Pop.

SID. There's a woman in the kitchen washing plastic forks with steel wool.

ARTIE. That's no woman, Pop. That's your daughter. *(Sid draws a blank. Helpfully.)* Ceil: Whose divorce shook a nation? That Ceil.

SID. Oh. *Oh.*

MORT. Leave it to Shirley ...

BELLA. What are you eating, Sid? Ceil has to go.

SID. A plum.

MORT. ... the most exotic thing on the menu she has to order. *(During the above, Artie begins to wrap food as Ceil returns from the kitchen.)*

CEIL. What are you doing, Artie?

ARTIE. I just thought I'd wrap some of this —

CEIL. *(Stopping him.)* No, darling, I'm doing it.

12

ARTIE. You said you were in a hurry. I don't mind. Really.

CEIL. *(Over "Really.")* That's very sweet of you, darling, but you're the one who's supposed to be "sitting," so sit. *(She presses him down onto the box.)*

MORT. *(Continuing his tirade.)* "You never try anything new," she says to me.

BELLA. *(Meaning, "Here he goes again!")* Uh!

MORT. "The hell with new," I says to her."Gimme a shrimp and lobster sauce combination plate any day." I was afraid of heartburn ...

MORT and ARTIE. ... Look what I wound up with! *(They look at one another for a beat; Artie exits to the bedroom.)*

MORT. Artie ...

BELLA. *(Quietly outraged.)* This is how a boy behaves his mother passes away? *(Mort shrugs helplessly.)* A boy yells out "liar" to the rabbi? In the middle of the funeral? I wanted to bury myself. You're his father, talk to him.

MORT. What do I say? Shirley did the talking. *You* talk to him.

BELLA. If *I* talk to him, I'll *say* something. This isn't normal, Morty, I'm telling you.

MORT. Ma, what do you want from me?!

CEIL. *(Intervening, while wrapping food.)* Morty, watch: I'm wrapping up all the food. You and Artie got food for a couple of days.

BELLA. You hear that, Morty? Ceil's wrapping up some lovely cold cuts. If I could bend my fingers ... I used to be such a good wrapper.

CEIL. I'm doing just fine, Ma.

BELLA. You're a *balebusteh* just like your mother. Remember when I was the *balebusteh*, Morty? Now it's your sister Ceil. What you got there, Ceil?

CEIL. A little bit of roast beef, a little whitefish, a little smoked sturgeon ...

BELLA. You hear that, Morty?

CEIL. Some turkey breast ...

BELLA. You hear that, Morty? Turkey breast. Slap together some rye bread, smear a little Russian dressing, you got yourself a tasty sandwich. *(Artie returns.)*

MORT. Artie'll make me sandwiches, right, Artie?

ARTIE. Yeah.

BELLA. That's right …

MORT. Artie'll take care of me, right, Artie?

BELLA. Of course he will.

ARTIE. You want something now?

BELLA. Isn't that funny, I was just gonna ask you the same thing. Are you hungry, Morty?

ARTIE. What do you want?

BELLA. Tell me.

ARTIE. I'll make you a sandwich.

BELLA. You want Momma to make you a sandwich? *(Mort shakes his head. Artie exits.)* You sure? You promise to tell me if you want something? *(Mort nods, takes out the Polaroid snapshot from his pocket and looks at it. Ceil exits. A beat.)* What are you looking at, darling? A picture? *(Mort nods.)* What kind of picture? *(Mort hands her the snapshot.)* Wait, darling, let me get my glasses … *(Bella goes into her handbag; Ceil returns with a Tupperware container.)*

CEIL. Tell Morty the cole slaw's in the orange Tupperware.

BELLA. Morty, just so you know, Ceil is putting the cole slaw in the orange Tupperware. My arthritis is so bad, I couldn't even burp the lid. *(Ceil "burps" the lid.)*

MORT. *(Barely audible.)* Shirley used to put leftovers in there.

CEIL. *(Whispers to Bella.)* What he say?

BELLA. *(Shrugs.)* Mortele, what did you say, darling? We couldn't hear you.

MORT. *(Still Softly.)* Shirley used to put leftovers in there.

BELLA. *(To Ceil, for corroboration.)* Shirley used to put leftovers in there? *(Mort nods sadly; Ceil returns to the kitchen.)* Aw, poor Morty. So many memories. *(Now wearing her glasses, she looks at the photo in puzzlement, then disbelief.)* What am I looking at, Morty? Oh, my God, Morty …

CEIL. *(Off.)* What?

BELLA. Get over here, Ceil, I can't believe this … *(Ceil enters; Bella hands her the photo.)*

CEIL. *(Looking at the picture.)* Morty! Oh, my God, I'm nauseous … *(She returns it to Bella, then takes it back for another look.)*

MORT. You ever see such a face? *(Artie returns.)*

CEIL. Where the hell did you get this?

ARTIE. Cousin Murray took it.

BELLA. Your retarded Cousin Murray?!

ARTIE. He takes his Polaroid everywhere.

BELLA. How'd he get away with bringing it into the chapel?

CEIL. Who would stop him, Ma? He's simple. He's got the mental age of an eight-year-old.

ARTIE. A pretty smart eight-year-old: My father had to give him ten bucks for that picture.

CEIL. Morty, you're kidding.

MORT. What a face! *(Bella snatches the photo from Ceil, who exits.)*

BELLA. What are you talking about, Morty, it doesn't even look like Shirley. *(To Artie.)* Does this look like your mother to you?

ARTIE. Never saw that corpse before in my life.

BELLA. Shirley did all kinds of crazy things to her hair but she never wore it like that. They brushed her all out! And that makeup! Since when did Shirley wear apricot lipstick?

MORT. That's how I want to remember Shirley.

BELLA. *(Returns the photo to Mort.)* Then, good. You hold on to it. *(A beat.)* I think it was barbaric putting Shirley in an open coffin like that in the first place.

MORT. *(Mostly to himself.)* So many people hadn't seen her for so long ...

BELLA. And that box!

MORT. ... It was always so hard making plans ...

ARTIE. *(To Bella.)* You mean The Supersaver?

BELLA. So plain, Artie, so flimsy. Those things are supposed to last.

MORT. Artie, when I go, I want you to bury me in the same kind of box you picked out for your mother. Nothing fancy.

ARTIE. Don't worry, Dad, when *you* die I'm gonna leave you on the F train. *(Artie laughs. Mort gestures to Sid as if to say, "What a mouth on that kid." Bella, meanwhile, has begun to uncover the mirror.)*

MORT. Leave it, Ma, I don't want you doing that.

BELLA. I can do it, I'm all right.

MORT. No. I don't want it off. Put it back.

BELLA. Shiva's over, Morty, time to take it off.

ARTIE. Grandma, why don't you let me do that later.

BELLA. How you gonna shave with the mirrors covered?

15

MORT. When I want to look at myself in the mirror …

BELLA. What, you growing a beard? Ceil, your brother's letting his beard grow.

CEIL. *(Off.)* Ma, if Morty doesn't feel like shaving …

BELLA. *(To Artie.)* Shave, darling, set an example for your father. I didn't realize you had such a little beard. *(Meaning it's more substantial than she thought.)*

ARTIE. I'll shave, we'll both shave.

BELLA. *Oy Gut,* Ceil, I got this feeling Morty and Artie are gonna be living like the Collyer brothers.

ARTIE. Aunt Ceil, what time's your date?

CEIL. *(Off.)* Ma, I'm gonna be late!

BELLA. You gonna sit like this forever? Shiva's over kids. Nobody else is gonna pay you a shiva call. There are things you've got to do: uncover the mirrors, shave. Go for a walk around the block. Take care of the clothes.

ARTIE. Grandma, we don't want to do that right now.

BELLA. All right, sit. *(A beat.)* You *know* you're supposed to burn the shoes.

ARTIE. Shoes?

BELLA. Don't look at me like I'm a witch, Artie, this is tradition. Jews have been burning dead people's shoes for millions of years.

ARTIE. Why?

BELLA. Look, when the Jews were in the desert, that's what they did. How'm *I* supposed to know?

MORT. Ma, if you burn one shoe …

BELLA. You gonna keep her shoes forever? Shirley doesn't need them anymore, Morty, where she is they run around barefoot.

CEIL. *(Off.)* Ma! *(Artie laughs in appreciation of Bella's joke.)*

BELLA. You gonna save all her things? All those lovely clothes … you gonna leave them in the closet? There are people who would flip over getting some of those clothes.

MORT. Who? Strangers on welfare? That's all Shirley would need: her beautiful garments on a rack in some thrift store.

BELLA. *(To Artie.)* Come, darling, we're gonna get rid of your mother's clothes and burn her shoes.

ARTIE. *(Restraining her.)* No, we are not!

BELLA. Who's gonna do it if not me? It would give me pleasure.

ARTIE. Stop! *(Ceil enters.)*

CEIL. Doesn't anybody around here care I got an important date tonight?!

ARTIE. *I* care! *I* care!

SID. *(Looking out the window.)* Artie?

ARTIE. *(Goes to Sid.)* Yeah, Pop.

SID. Look at that: right across the street: a perfect park. Nobody can say your grandpa doesn't have a nose for parking spaces.

ARTIE. You're the best, Pop.

SID. Oh, you should've seen me at the wheel. I pulled into that space like in a glove. Smooth as ice!

BELLA. *(To Ceil.)* What do you know about this fella tonight?

CEIL. Spoke to him once on the phone.

BELLA. And?

CEIL. Speaks English.

BELLA. And?

CEIL. Ma!

SID. *(To Artie.)* When you gonna let me take you for a ride in the cab?

ARTIE. Soon, Pop. Whenever you want.

BELLA. *(To Mort.)* Maybe your sister's gonna bring home a new brother-in-law for you, Morty. Would you like that?

CEIL. Ma …

BELLA. I'm only pulling your leg, Ceil. So sensitive …

SID. *(To Artie.)* Tell your grandma how I worked rush-hour traffic.

ARTIE. Like a genius.

SID. You hear that, Bella? He says like a genius.

BELLA. Very nice, Sid.

SID. *(Excitedly.)* I overtook that Greyhound one-two-three. Remember, Artie?

ARTIE. Uh-huh.

SID. It was breathtaking. *(A beat.)* Bella, my nitroglycerine.

BELLA. You're not getting a heart attack.

SID. How do you know?!

BELLA. Your lips aren't blue.

SID. I feel burning!

BELLA. I'm not giving you your nitroglycerine unless you promise to let it melt under your tongue like you're supposed to! *(To*

Artie.) He chews them!

SID. Where is it?

BELLA. In my bag. Help yourself.

ARTIE. Pop, I'll get it for you.

BELLA. Let him. He needs the exercise. You've been running around all week. *(Sid exits.)*

CEIL. *(Calls to Sid as he goes.)* Daddy, get our coats while you're at it. We gotta get out of here, Ma. *(She exits to kitchen.)*

BELLA. What do you want from *me?!* Everybody's jumping down my throat. *(A beat.)* Artie, Artie, Artie … Friends you can have plenty of, but a mother? One in a lifetime. *(Pause. She examines the fabric on the new furniture.)* Your mother picked a very impractical fabric, darling. She had lots of opinions, your mother may she rest in peace. Maybe if she bothered to *cook* a little more often, she'd be alive today. Cleaning, *that* she could do. You couldn't put down a glass of *water* without Shirley pulling out a coaster. That's the kind of woman your mother was, Artie, may she rest in peace: a very particular person.

CEIL. *(Off.)* All right, Ma, enough with Shirley already!

BELLA. What did I say? "A very particular person"! I can't say "a very particular person"? *(Sid returns.)*

SID. What was I looking for?

BELLA. Where did you go? You wanted your nitroglycerine! I said it's in my bag! My bag is right here! Maybe if you paid attention, Sid, you wouldn't forget. *(Takes a bottle from her handbag and gives one pill to Sid.)* And don't chew it. Leave it under your tongue. *(Ceil returns.)*

CEIL. Pop, what you do with our coats?

SID. What coats?

CEIL. I asked you to bring in the coats!

SID. *(Chewing the tablet.)* I didn't hear nothing about coats!

BELLA. Sidney, are you chewing?

CEIL. God!

ARTIE. I'll get the coats. *(He exits.)*

CEIL. *(Exiting to kitchen.)* Oy, is that an Artie … *(Bella exits to the bedroom. Sid and Mort, left alone, sit for a moment in silence.)*

SID. Mort?

MORT. Yeah, Pop? *(Pause.)*

18

SID. Mort ... *(A beat.)* You never *could* park. *(A beat. Artie returns with the coats.)*

ARTIE. Here's your coat, Pop. *(Bella enters with an armful of Shirley's clothing on hangers and lays it out on the sofa.)*

MORT. Ma, what the hell are you doing?!

BELLA. Years from now you'll thank me, Morty. *(She begins to fold clothing.)*

ARTIE. Grandma, who asked you to do that?!

BELLA. *Some*body's got to do this, sweetheart ...

MORT. Ma, no!

CEIL. *(Over "sweetheart" ...)* Ma, what are you starting?!

BELLA. There are things that have to be done ...

CEIL. I told you I got to go!

BELLA. ... and I'm the one that has to do them.

MORT. You want to fold up a whole lifetime and put it in a shopping bag?!

BELLA. This is gonna take more than one shopping bag, my son.

ARTIE. You can do this some other time!

CEIL. Artie's right, Ma ...

MORT. You're killing me, Ma ...

CEIL. ... It doesn't have to be done right this minute!

MORT. ... Is that what you want? You want to kill me?!

BELLA. All of a sudden I'm your enemy, Morty? I want to help you!

MORT. THIS ISN'T HELPING ME!

BELLA. *(Throws down the clothes.)* Save the clothes! I don't care. They're not gonna bring Shirley back!

CEIL. Ma, enough! Can't you see you're upsetting Morty?

BELLA. I'm concerned.

ARTIE. Don't be concerned.

CEIL. Ma, come. *(Spots a garment of interest; a beat.)* Is that Shirley's fur jacket?

BELLA. Try it on. Be my guest. *(Ceil is considering it.)*

MORT. NO!

CEIL. All right, all right. Not now.

BELLA. *(To Mort.)* Pull yourself together! My God!

CEIL. *(Still eyeing the jacket.)* Don't worry, Morty, we'll stop by tomorrow. We'll take care of everything. *(Helping Sid into his coat.)*

Gimme your arm, Pop.

SID. Where we going?

CEIL. Home.

SID. What about our shiva call? We had a shiva call.

BELLA. *(Putting on her coat.) This* is the shiva call, Sid. We're sitting with Morty, remember? We've been here every day this week, remember? Shirley passed away.

SID. Shirley?! I don't believe it!

BELLA. In a restaurant, a Chinese restaurant.

SID. Shirley was a young woman …

CEIL. Let's go home, Daddy. *(Bella sneaks a peek at herself in the mirror.)*

BELLA. Well, Morty? Artie? Look at my two little bachelors … *(Goes to Mort.)* We must go on living, Mortele. Come, walk me to the elevator.

MORT. My life is over Ma. This is it, this is the end.

BELLA. Oh, Morty, don't say that …

CEIL. How can you talk like that, Morty…?

ARTIE. *(Over "talk like that, Morty…?")* Would you stop with that already?! You've got a good twenty-five, maybe thirty years left.

MORT. *(A beat; worried.)* That's all?

BELLA. Sid?

CEIL. I'm getting him, Ma. Oh, Morty, before I forget: your thank-you notes. *(Hands Mort a box.)*

ARTIE. I'll take them. *(Mort passes the box to Artie.)*

CEIL. Morty, all you have to do is sign your name. The note is printed nice, like a wedding invitation.

ARTIE. He's not gonna do it, I'll do it.

CEIL. Look, Morty: the address book. I checked off the names of the people who came in black Magic Marker. *(Ceil passes the book to Mort, who gives it to Artie.)*

BELLA. I would sign them for you, sweetheart, you *know* that, but my knuckles won't let me.

CEIL. Morty, are you listening?

ARTIE. I'll take care of it.

CEIL. This is important, Artie.

ARTIE. Okay.

CEIL. People have to get thanked.

ARTIE. All right.

CEIL. You have to acknowledge.

ARTIE. I know.

CEIL. Very important. People go out of their way, you have to thank them. I'm gonna remind you.

ARTIE. I'll remember.

BELLA. *(Hugging Artie.)* Oh Artie ... my little Artie ... such *tsuris. (They kiss.)* Try to find that ticket, darling, I'm gonna be up the whole night. *(Leading Mort out the door.)* Come, Mort. Be careful with your father, Ceil. There's a coffee table here I didn't even see.

CEIL. *(As Bella and Mort exit.)* No, I'm gonna let him walk in to it and kill himself. God, Ma! *(Goes to Artie, gives him her cheek to kiss.)* Be strong, Artie. *(He kisses her cheek.)*

ARTIE. *(Handing her a thank-you note.)* Thank you. *(Ceil snatches the note from him.)*

SID. Artie?

ARTIE. Yeah, Pop.

SID. I lost my mother Artie, I was fifty-seven years old.

ARTIE. Yeah.

SID. Not a kid like you. Fifty-seven years old but I cried like a baby. I just didn't have the strength. Better this should happen when you're young and you got the strength. It's a gift, Artie, believe me. *(He kisses Artie; Artie hugs him.)*

CEIL. Pop, come on, Mom's holding the elevator.

ARTIE. Goodbye, Pop.

SID. Where did I park, Ceil?

CEIL. *You* didn't park, Daddy. *I* did. *I* drove.

SID. I parked like a dream.

CEIL. *I* drove, Pop. I *parked.* They took away your license, remember?

SID. *(A beat; as they exit:)* Ah, fuck 'em. Fuck the State. *(They're gone. Artie, alone, silently surveys the room. In a few beats, Mort returns, shuffling despondently with his hands in his pockets. They eye one another uncomfortably. Silence.)*

ARTIE. *(Sings.)* "Quarter to three ... there's no one in the place ... 'cept you and me ... " *(Mort is not amused. Pause.)* Dad? *(Pause.)* Some week, huh? *(Pause.)* Went fast. *(Pause.)* Soon I'll be as old as Pop talking about what happened when I was seventeen.

MORT. What am I gonna do with all that closet space?

ARTIE. We keep moving but Mommy's stuck somewhere. It's like I'm watching her in the waves at Coney Island, getting smaller and smaller. This game she played with me in the waves.

MORT. Your mother was funny. *(Begins laughing to himself.)*

ARTIE. She makes believe she's drowning and I cry hysterically.

MORT. She always made me laugh, your mother.

ARTIE. Yeah. See, I'm a little-little boy, maybe four, and she swims away, does a backstroke, way out, where the water's too deep, she won't let me go out that far, but I see her face —

MORT. What a face!

ARTIE. That young-Mommy face? Wet and shiny? Smiling at me? Rising away on a wave ... And she calls to me ...

MORT. *(Interrupting.)* What a sense of humor! We were in the supermarket once, must've been Waldbaum's, in the aisle with all the cereals ...

ARTIE. Dad, listen: She calls to me ...

MORT. ... and I was pushing the cart ... and your mother said ... *(He can't remember.)*

ARTIE. "Goodbyyeee forevverr!"

MORT. *(Still trying to remember.)* She said something ...

ARTIE. Dad...?

MORT. Something funny. Something so funny it cracked me up.

ARTIE. Then she swims back and tells me everything's okay, it was only a game.

MORT. You could be sure if it was coming out of her mouth, it was funny. She had a real talent with words. She could put together sentences of all kinds, your mother. I wish I could remember some of the stuff she said. I should've written it down. *(During the above, Artie abandons his attempt to tell his story and tries to clear away some furniture by himself.)*

ARTIE. Dad, we really should do something about the house.

MORT. What's wrong with it?

ARTIE. *(Struggling with a chair.)* Help me with this? Dad? Help me.

MORT. *(Regarding the clothing.)* What class your mother had! What flair! The way she filled these things out with that body of hers! God, she was something else in the love department your mother, Artie.

ARTIE. That's great news, Dad, thanks for telling me.

MORT. *(Holding up a dress.)* Oh, your mother got pizza juice on this. Made me open up the store on a Sunday morning to dry clean it. You see a stain?

ARTIE. Nope.

MORT. Of course not. I'm a professional. *(He comes across a red sequined dress.)* Oh! Remember this? I bet you don't remember when your mother —

ARTIE. She wore that to my bar mitzvah.

MORT. That's right! I'll never forget how she looked that night: chandelier earrings ... high-heeled shoes ... her hair in a French flip. God, she was a vision. I watched her on the dance floor doing the "Alley Cat." She shimmered! Like fire she was! *(Hums a few bars of the "Alley Cat" song* while holding the dress against his chest. A beat.)* You can't give something like this away

ARTIE. You can't save souvenirs either.

MORT. Never mind, you. You're too young. You don't know what love is. You know how much this thing cost? Cost me a fortune. Whatever your mother wanted she got: this dress, shoes that had to be dyed to match perfect, a beaded bag she hocked me a *chinik* for, I doubt she used it more than once. *(Examining the dress.)* Look at this construction. Look how it's stitched. Even dry cleaning couldn't hurt it. Let's see how it held up. Try it on.

ARTIE. What?

MORT. Just slip it over your head a minute.

ARTIE. Why?

MORT. I'm curious.

ARTIE. You want me to wear this?

MORT. What are you getting so touchy? Who's asking you to wear it? Just try it on. *(Artie takes the dress from Mort, holds it up.)*

ARTIE. Here, how does it look?

MORT. No, no, not like that. That's no way to see how something looks, how well it hangs. That's the trouble with beading of any kind: The garment loses shape.

ARTIE. So you put it on.

* See Special Note on Songs and Recordings on copyright page.

MORT. Me? You gotta be kidding. I couldn't fit into this, I'm too broad. Believe me, if I could, I would. You're lucky: You it would fit.

ARTIE. What are you talking about?!

MORT. *(Angry.)* When do I ever ask you for a goddamn thing? Hm? I ask you one simple thing ...

ARTIE. I'm not gonna put on my mother's dress just because you want me to!

MORT. It would give your dad such pleasure, Artie, such a kick.

ARTIE. To see me in a dress?!

MORT. Not just any dress, your mother's spitfire dress! She wore this to your bar mitzvah, Artie, to your bar mitzvah! We're not talking *schmatte* here, we're talking something I would give my eyeteeth to see shimmering again. Your mother wore this dress, Artie. On her body. She danced in this dress. She shook and shimmered in it. She sweated in this dress. This dress *was* your mother, Artie. *(He lays the dress across Artie's lap; Artie considers it for a moment, then stands to put it on.)* Atta boy.

ARTIE. For one minute.

MORT. That's all I'm asking. *(Artie begins to step into the dress.)*

ARTIE. It's not gonna fit.

MORT. So, I'll have it taken in.

ARTIE. I don't know, Dad ... *(Adjusting the dress.)* Well? How does it look?

MORT. *(Enthralled.)* Fabulous!

ARTIE. You're just saying that.

MORT. Sweetheart, you look exquisite!

ARTIE. Zip me up? *(Mort does.)*

MORT. Turn around. *(Meaning in a circle.)*

ARTIE. Do I have to?

MORT. Come on ... *(Artie turns.)* Oh, yes! Beautiful! Again! *(Artie, beginning to revel in the dress, spins around again and again; he and Mort are giddy.)* Shimmer! That's right, shimmer! *(Mort puts his hands on Artie's hips and sings the "Alley Cat" song* as he and Artie do the dance steps. Their singing and dancing become increasingly frenetic as they wind their way through the living room. They collapse, laughing, on the sofa.)*

* See Special Note on Songs and Recordings on copyright page.

24

ARTIE. This thing is heavy. It pulls a little bit in the shoulders.

MORT. I can let that out. Whatever you want. *(Mort puts his arm around Artie and turns on the television. Artie prepares to stand.)* Sit with me a minute. *(A beat.)*

ARTIE. Okay. *(He settles back into the sofa. Mort, his arm around Artie, rests his head on Artie's shoulder. Mort laughs at something on TV. Pause. Artie gets up.)*

MORT. Where you going? We're just getting comfortable.

ARTIE. I thought I'd make us something to eat.

MORT. Now *there's* an idea! *(Artie, still wearing the dress, exits to the kitchen. Mort, humming, takes off his trousers and folds them over the back of a chair. Artie returns with a tray of food and utensils.)* Wow! Look at all that stuff! *(Artie sets the food down on the table. Mort stands sampling the food with his fingers.)* Mmm...! Cole slaw ... potato salad ... macaroni salad ...

ARTIE. Use a fork.

MORT. ... pickled herring in cream sauce ... mmmm ...

ARTIE. Come on, sit down, use a fork. Here's a plate. Here's a napkin. Help yourself. *(He sniffs a container of cottage cheese for freshness, makes a terrible face and sets it aside.)*

MORT. Your mother always did that. What a nose on her! Never failed. One whiff, she could tell you whether or not the thing was sour. *(Artie pours two cups of Tab; Mort eyes the soda can nostalgically.)* Tab ... *(A beat.)* I don't know what to have. What should I eat? How about you?

ARTIE. I'm gonna have whitefish on a bagel. *(Begins to slice a bagel.)*

MORT. No, don't do that. You'll cut yourself. *(Takes the bagel and knife from Artie.)*

ARTIE. I can do it.

MORT. *(Slicing the bagel.)* I don't want you to cut yourself; your mother was always cutting herself. *(Returns the sliced bagel to Artie, who prepares a sandwich as Mort watches.)* What do you do? You just smear the fish on the bagel?

ARTIE. That's right.

MORT. What about the bones?

ARTIE. You pick out the bones.

MORT. One by one?

25

ARTIE. That's right.

MORT. They're so tiny. Hey, you do that good.

ARTIE. *(Passes the fish and a bagel to Mort.)* Here. Help yourself

MORT. Isn't that funny? I never knew what happened to the bones You see how good she was to me? *(Smearing fish on the bagel.)* Now I have to smear on the fish and pick out the bones. Right?

ARTIE. Uh-huh.

MORT. Boy, she was some cook, wasn't she.

ARTIE. Yeah.

MORT. What an imagination on her. How about that meat loaf!

ARTIE. Yeah!

MORT. She'd throw in things you'd never in a million years expect to taste good together and they'd come out spectacular. Like a can of peas she'd throw in. Who would've thought of that? That's a talent, isn't it, to throw things together and have them come out like a gourmet meal? Remember she'd throw together all those different things and put it in the oven?

ARTIE. Yeah …

MORT. Remember those casseroles she made?

ARTIE. Yeah.

MORT. What did she call them?

ARTIE. The casseroles?

MORT. Yeah, she had a name for them.

ARTIE. "Casseroles."

MORT. Right, what did she call them?

ARTIE. She called the casseroles "casseroles." *(A beat. Mort i annoyed.)*

MORT. Always the wiseguy.

ARTIE. What's the matter?

MORT. Always with the smart answers.

ARTIE. That's what she called her casseroles: "casseroles"!

MORT. *(Enraged; overlap.)* You talk to your teachers like this Hm? Is this how you talk to your teachers, or just to your fathe you talk like this?

ARTIE. She called them "casseroles"!

MORT. Never mind, you little bastard. I ask you a simple question, I don't want any of that wiseguy shit.

ARTIE. I answered your question!

26

MORT. Look, you've been blasé about this whole thing —

ARTIE. What?!

MORT. ... from the very beginning.

ARTIE. What are you talking about?!

MORT. The little jokes, the comments. Making a scene at the funeral?!

ARTIE. Who made a scene?! *You* almost jumped in the hole with her!

MORT. Never mind about me!

ARTIE. I could've been a lucky orphan: two birds with one stone! *(Mort pushes his bagel into Artie's face.)*Hey!

MORT. You don't stop! You don't give a damn what happened!

ARTIE. How can you say that?

MORT. I can and I *do. (Hands Artie a napkin.)* Wipe your face; you've got fish.

ARTIE. *(Wiping his face.) I* was the one who made the phone calls, who picked out the box —

MORT. I haven't seen you cry once all week.

ARTIE. Is that what you want? Well, I haven't gotten around to that yet. I'm new at this, okay?!

MORT. If somebody's hungry, they eat. If they're sad, they cry.

ARTIE. You're saying I'm not sad?

MORT. Starting up with the rabbi?! That's sad?!

ARTIE. He never even met her! He's making up all these lies about her!

MORT. It was a funeral! You're supposed to say nice things!

ARTIE. And everybody's sitting there listening to this garbage, nodding their heads, saying, "Yeah that was Shirley all right!" And I'm saying, "No! No! That's not who she was!" *(The doorbell rings.)*

MORT. Then who was she, hm, wiseguy? *(Doorbell. Calls.)* Coming! *(To Artie.)* Get the door.

ARTIE. Why don't you?

MORT. I'm wearing underwear.

ARTIE. So what? I'm wearing a dress. *(Doorbell.)*

MORT. You're closer. *(Doorbell again and again.)*

ARTIE. *(Approaching the door.)* Okay, okay ... *(Artie opens the door. Standing there is his dead mother, Shirley, her face and hair caked with dirt, her shroud tattered, encrusted with mud and stained with grass.)* Ma!

MORT. Shirley! *(Shirley speaks as she makes her way, on sore feet, through the living room to the bathroom.)*

SHIRLEY. Look ... I don't even want to talk about it ... I've just gotta jump in the shower ... *(As she enters the bathroom.)* Oh, the furniture came! Good! *(She closes the door behind her. In a moment, while Mort and Artie remain incredulous, the shower is turned on.)*

MORT. *(Very frightened.)* Artie? What the hell is going on, Artie? *(Artie, giggling nervously, shakes his head.)* See, I just saw your mother ... *(Points to the front door, then to the bathroom.)*

ARTIE. Uh-huh.

MORT. You, too?

ARTIE. *(Nods.)* Daddy, what should we do? *(Shirley, in the shower, is singing "Send in the Clowns."*)*

MORT. Shhh ... Now I think I hear her singing "Send in the Clowns."

ARTIE. She is.

MORT. *(Trying to make sense of what he hears.)* You know, she loved that song, your mother. I never understood what the words meant, but whenever she heard Sinatra sing it, she'd get all choked up. Listen to that: She's in tune and everything.

ARTIE. Uh-huh.

MORT. Artie, you think your mother's gonna haunt us by coming over and taking showers? *(Artie shrugs. The shower is turned off.)*

SHIRLEY. *(Off.)* Boys?

MORT. Shhh ...

SHIRLEY. *(Off.)* Boys? Did I get any mail?

MORT. Your mother wants to know if she got any mail.

ARTIE. *(A beat; calls.)* Uh, yeah. Bills, mostly. Oh, and the new *People* came.

SHIRLEY. *(Off.)* Oh, good ... *(Enters, drying her hair with a towel.)* There is nothing worse than walking around with dirty hair. I feel like a new person. Ah! Now you can kiss me. *(Artie tentatively approaches, Mort restrains him.)* No kiss? This is the kind of welcome I get? *(A beat; insulted.)* Well, don't think I haven't noticed the dress, Artie.

* See Special Note on Songs and Recordings on copyright page.

ARTIE. Oh, this …

SHIRLEY. Yeah, "this." You let him walk around like that, Morty?

MORT. He has wild ideas.

ARTIE. It was your idea! Ma, Daddy made me put it on!

MORT. *(Cutting him off.)* Ah, what the hell: You got to admit, he carries it well. *(He laughs; Shirley does, too. The utter naturalness of their sharing a laugh causes him to pause.)* Shirley, is that really you?

SHIRLEY. Yeah, Mort, it's me.

MORT. Now what do you mean by "you"?

SHIRLEY. I mean, me.

MORT. Did you come to take me with you?

SHIRLEY. Take you where, Mort?, nobody's going anywhere.

MORT. Shirley! I don't believe it! You're here talking to me!

SHIRLEY. Yes, Mort.

MORT. Artie, your mother's home!

ARTIE. Yeah! I know! *(Mort pulls Artie into a three-way embrace.)*

MORT. Oh, Shirley, Shirley, Shirley …

SHIRLEY. This is more like it!

MORT. I knew you'd get it straightened out sooner or later. Leave it to your mother, hm, Artie?

ARTIE. Yeah! *(Suddenly chilled, he recoils.)*

SHIRLEY. What.

ARTIE. You're cold.

MORT. *(He, too, recoils.)* Boy, you *are* cold.

SHIRLEY. *(Self-conscious.)* I am?

MORT. Here, put something on … *(Meaning her clothes on the sofa.)*

SHIRLEY. *(Seeing the clothes.)* My clothes! What are my clothes doing out here?! Look at this! Everything's gonna get wrinkled! *(She starts to put things back on hangers.)*

MORT. I told them you wouldn't like it. Shirley, let me look at you! You look great!

SHIRLEY. How could I?

MORT. Artie, doesn't your mother look beautiful?

ARTIE. Actually she looks a little pale.

MORT. What does a kid know? To me you look wonderful.

SHIRLEY. To you, you're prejudiced.

MORT. Maybe a little. *(He takes her hand, is struck again by its peculiar coldness and warms it by rubbing it between his hands.)*

29

ARTIE. So, Ma, how'd you get here?

SHIRLEY. Don't ask.

MORT. Yeah, Shirley, what'd you do? Walk?

SHIRLEY. Yeah, I walked.

MORT. On foot?

SHIRLEY. Yeah, on foot.

MORT. From all the way out on the Island?

SHIRLEY. Uh-huh.

MORT. What'd you do, take the B.Q.E.?

SHIRLEY. The B.Q.E., the L.I.E., the Belt, the Van Wyck ...

MORT. Why didn't you call me?! I could've picked you up!

SHIRLEY. Morty ...

MORT. Since when do you stand on ceremony with me, Shirley?

SHIRLEY. I didn't have a cent!

MORT. Oh, my poor baby ...

SHIRLEY. God, look at this place! The dust! *(Tidying up.)* What moron burned a hole in my finish? It's ruined.

MORT. Shirley you'd've gotten a kick out of all the fancy baskets that came. *(Picks up a jam jar.)* Want some "Gooseberry Preserves"?

SHIRLEY. Throw that out, we're never gonna eat that shit. *(Artie laughs. She takes dying flowers from a vase.)* Who sent these?

ARTIE. Your boss.

SHIRLEY. *Goyim.* All they know is flowers. *(She hands them to Mort to get rid of; he hands them to Artie.)* I can't believe this mess! I was counting on you, Morty!

MORT. What!

SHIRLEY. I work my whole life to make a nice home, I'm gone a couple of days and you let the house fall apart! *(She starts for the hall closet.)*

MORT. *(Thinking she's leaving.)* No, don't go! We'll fix it up! *(She takes the vacuum cleaner out of the closet.)* What are you shlepping! Character! *(To Artie.)* Help your mother. *(He does.)*

SHIRLEY. *(Unveiling mirrors, etc.)* I don't know how the two of you can breathe in here! The dust, the furniture ...

ARTIE. *(To Mort.)* See? *(To Shirley.)* That's what I told him, Ma, I told him we can't keep all the old stuff, he wouldn't listen to me.

MORT. *(Over, " ... he wouldn't listen to me")* All right, all right ...

we'll get rid of it.

SHIRLEY. Into the hall. Let the super deal with it. *(To Mort.)* And I want you to shave. I don't like you looking so scruffy.

MORT. That'll make you happy?

SHIRLEY. Yes, Mort, very happy

MORT. Whatever makes you happy. Boy, this business gave us a real scare, didn't it?

ARTIE. It sure did.

MORT. The house feels like a home again! *(He snuggles up to her and recoils from her coldness again.)* You sure you don't want a sweater?

SHIRLEY. I'm fine.

MORT. Artie, get your mother a sweater. *(Artie goes. To Shirley.)* Don't go away.

SHIRLEY. I won't. *(Mort goes to the bathroom. Shirley sits alone for a beat contemplating the gravity of her situation. Mort is shaving while humming the "Alley Cat" song.* Soon, Artie returns with a sweater and drapes it over his mother's shoulders.)*

ARTIE. So, Ma, what's going on?

SHIRLEY. What do you mean?

ARTIE. Come on, you can tell me. Is this a visitation?

SHIRLEY. A "visitation"? Who's visiting? I'm home.

ARTIE. But, Ma ... You're dead.

SHIRLEY. So? Aren't you glad to see me?

ARTIE. Of course I'm glad to see you.

SHIRLEY. Then leave it at that. Don't make waves.

ARTIE. I'd almost forgotten what you looked like, you know that? And your voice? I tried for hours last night to conjure it up in my head? I fell asleep without even coming close.

SHIRLEY. Oh, sweetheart ...

ARTIE. Ma, all week long, ever since this happened, it's been so crazy ...

SHIRLEY. I'm so sorry, honey, just when you needed me the most and I wasn't here to be with you.

ARTIE. I kept hoping you'd come home and make everything right again.

* See Special Note on Songs and Recordings on copyright page.

31

SHIRLEY. *(Simply.)* And now I'm here. Mommy's home, Artie. Everything's gonna be okay.

ARTIE. I missed you so much.

SHIRLEY. Well, you don't have to miss me anymore. *(Mort, still shaving, pops in from the bathroom.)*

MORT. Shirley?

SHIRLEY. Yeah, Mort?

MORT. How about you cook for me that meat loaf thing?

SHIRLEY. My casserole? Sure. *(More vindication for Artie. Mort returns to the bathroom. Artie follows Shirley around the room as she continues to clean it up.)*

ARTIE. So ... Ma ... *(A beat.)* What are your plans?

SHIRLEY. Well, I've got this house to put together. First, we get rid of all the old furniture ...

ARTIE. Uh-huh.

SHIRLEY. Then, I'm gonna dust, polish, vacuum, do the floors, take apart the kitchen, arrange the new stuff. I promise you, sweetheart, when I get done with this place ... everything's gonna be perfect! *(She blows out the memorial candle. A recording of the "Alley Cat" song* takes us into the blackout.)*

* See Special Note on Songs and Recordings on copyright page.

ACT TWO

At rise: early the next day. Most of the old furniture has been moved out of the living room; what remains is a motley arrangement of the new furniture, still in its wrapping, and a few favorite pieces from the former set. Shirley and Artie have begun to unwrap a new chair but she has stopped to scrutinize something he has shown her: the Polaroid snapshot of her dead self. Artie stands nearby, drinking coffee, taking delight in her reaction. Mort is contentedly dozing on the sofa. After a beat:

SHIRLEY. Who took this, your Cousin Murray?
ARTIE. Yup.
SHIRLEY. *(She shakes her head, "It figures.")* What they did to my hair ... unforgivable. *(She hands it back to Artie and resumes unwrapping a chair, etc. He helps her.)* And that shroud! Like for an old lady. That's not how I wanted to go at all.
ARTIE. What do I know about shrouds? It was the first time I had to shop for one.
SHIRLEY. You? Where was your father?
ARTIE. Oh, he wouldn't come into the room. You know, The Chamber of Horrors in the basement of the funeral chapel? Where they have the coffins and everything? I hope you're not offended, I picked the one on sale.
SHIRLEY. A box is a box.
ARTIE. That's what I said.
SHIRLEY. Your father let you do all that awful stuff by yourself?
ARTIE. Somebody had to; he was in no shape to do anything. I even had to make the phone calls. "Hi, this is Shirley and Morty's kid, Artie? Remember my mother? Well, uh, guess what?" I lose my mother and end up telling two hundred and fifty people how sorry I am to have to break it to them.

SHIRLEY. That's not right. You shouldn't've had to do all that. You're just a kid.

ARTIE. See, now that's what I thought. I mean, didn't all the other animals help out Bambi? Everybody's treating me like it's my fault or something.

SHIRLEY. Who is?

ARTIE. I don't know ... Dad, Grandma. *(A beat.)* See, there was this ... minor incident.

SHIRLEY. What kind of minor incident?

ARTIE. At the service. The rabbi was one of those fill-in-the blank kind of rabbis? He even called you "Sally" a few times.

SHIRLEY. You're kidding.

ARTIE. No, I yelled out your name, correcting him, and Grandma shushed me.

SHIRLEY. *(Amused.)* Uy ...

ARTIE. Anyway, he never even met you and he's saying all these corny things about you. You would've hated it, Ma. He made you sound like *any*body's mother. Well, it was getting me mad sitting there and listening to that stuff. But I couldn't control myself.

SHIRLEY. So what did you do?

ARTIE. I called him a liar.

SHIRLEY. *(Enjoying this.)* You did? What did you do, you just yelled it out?

ARTIE. Uh-huh.

SHIRLEY. So what happened?

ARTIE. He stopped the service.

SHIRLEY. Yeah?

ARTIE. "If you think you can do a better job," he said, "why don't you come up here and do it yourself?" So, I did. I mean, I got up and went to the microphone and looked out and saw the faces of everybody I ever knew in my entire life and then I looked at the box ... And then this funny thing happened.

SHIRLEY. What.

ARTIE. I opened my mouth to speak ...

SHIRLEY. Yeah...?

ARTIE. And nothing came out. I couldn't speak. I didn't know what to say. I just stood there. With everybody looking. And I didn't know what to say. So I ran out and waited by the car till it was over.

SHIRLEY. Oh, sweetheart ...

ARTIE. Ma, ever since this happened ... You know what it's like? *(Shirley shakes her head.)* It's like we're in the ocean, you and me. I close my eyes and we're back in the ocean. Remember? At Coney Island?

SHIRLEY. Tell me.

ARTIE. I'm a little-little boy. And we're playing in the water, splashing around, chasing the foam, having a great time, then all of a sudden, you swim away! You tell me to stay by the shore and you swim, way out, where the water's too deep for me, you won't let me go out that far. So I do as you tell me, I stay by the shore, but I see your face, wet and shiny, smiling at me, getting smaller and smaller, rising away on a wave. And you call to me. Remember, Ma? You call to me ...

SHIRLEY. "Goodbyyeee forevverr!"

ARTIE. Yeah! "Goodbyyeee forevverr!" And I panic. "No, Mommy!"

SHIRLEY. *(Laughs affectionately.)* Oh, Artie ...

ARTIE. That's funny?, making believe you're being washed out to sea?!

SHIRLEY. It was a game!

ARTIE. I think I'm never gonna see you again! I cry. I get hysterical. Strangers ask me if I'm lost. I can't catch my breath. The tears are so thick I can't see you anymore. I can't see anything. I think my heart is gonna stop 'cause who's gonna take care of me if you're gone? And then you come back!

SHIRLEY. See?

ARTIE. You swim back and you're laughing! You're laughing!

SHIRLEY. You're mad because I didn't drown?, what?

ARTIE. What kind of trick is that to play on a kid?

SHIRLEY. Trick? I always swam back to you, didn't I? And picked you up out of the water and told you it was just a game, everything was all right? Didn't I?

ARTIE. Yeah, but why did you do that to me?

SHIRLEY. Why? I was playing with you!

ARTIE. No, no, I think you enjoyed seeing me get hysterical.

SHIRLEY. Why would I enjoy seeing you get hysterical?

ARTIE. I don't know, to see how much I'd miss you? *(They look at one another for a beat. Mort stirs, panics for a moment thinking Shirley is gone, then sees her and beams with pleasure that she's still there.)*

MORT. Shirley! *(She smiles and waves at him. Mort wakens and stretches noisily. Artie drinks the rest of the coffee.)*

SHIRLEY. You're drinking too much coffee; I don't like you drinking so much coffee.

ARTIE. I want to stay up with you. If you're not gonna sleep, neither am I. What if I fall asleep and wake up and you're gone? *(He exits to the kitchen to make a fresh pot.)*

SHIRLEY. *(To herself; distressed.) Sleep?* I forgot all about it …

MORT. *(Brightly; singsong.)* Hi-i.

SHIRLEY. *(Preoccupied; resumes puttering.)* Hi.

MORT. Look at you.

SHIRLEY. What.

MORT. *(Romantically.)* I can't keep my eyes open and you're all over the place. I drift in and out, I see a hundred Shirleys. Shirley polishing. Shirley vacuuming. Shirley shlepping furniture. You're everywhere.

SHIRLEY. Morty, I *can't* sleep.

MORT. Of course you can't sleep. You're all wired up.

SHIRLEY. No, I can't sleep.

MORT. You never knew how to sit still. Always doing something. You've gotta learn how to relax, Shirley. *(He leads her to the sofa.)*

SHIRLEY. No sleep, no dreams … No more dreams, Mort! I had such good dreams.

MORT. Shhh … Listen to me: just now, I dreamed we went to Hawaii.

SHIRLEY. Hawaii?!

MORT. I got you there, once and for all. What a relief, hm?

SHIRLEY. I always wanted to go to Hawaii.

MORT. I know! I was feeling terrible.

SHIRLEY. Ever since my first luau at Hawaii Kai. We went from *Fiddler on the Roof* to pineapple everything.

MORT. Oh, the place was paradise, Shirley. Everything we dreamed it would be.

SHIRLEY. Yeah?

MORT. Sun as big as the moon. Water like Saran Wrap. These Hawaiians, they don't know from clouds. *(She laughs.)* I'm telling you, we were so tan I didn't recognize us. We wore flowers 'round our necks like natives. You know what you looked like? Pink flowers and a tan? Wow.

SHIRLEY. *(Wistfully.)* Oh ... *(A dreamy pause.)*

MORT. Why don't we do it?

SHIRLEY. What.

MORT. Once and for all: Hawaii.

SHIRLEY. Morty, we can't do that ...

MORT. Why not? We'll hula till the sun sets! *(She laughs.)* Let's do it, Shirley! We'll take a trip! You and me!

SHIRLEY. I can't.

MORT. We'll take a cruise 'round the islands! A cruise, Shirley! It's like a floating Catskills!

SHIRLEY. You go. You do it.

MORT. What do you mean? By myself? I wouldn't dream of it. Come with me!

SHIRLEY. Things are different now, Morty. Dreams change.

MORT. All you have to do is get on a plane.

SHIRLEY. I'm not getting on any plane.

MORT. You could use a vacation. We both could. After what we've been through?!

SHIRLEY. Morty, I can't take a vacation.

MORT. Why not?

SHIRLEY. You know why not.

MORT. That? I don't give a damn about that. You're here, aren't you?

SHIRLEY. Yeah, I'm home. Where I belong. As long as you and Artie want me, I'll be here. But vacations? No, not anymore, That's over for me, Morty. Which doesn't mean it has to be over for you.

MORT. Would you think about it at least?

SHIRLEY. There's nothing to think about. I can't. I'm sorry.

MORT. *(Pause.)* It was a wonderful dream, Shirley.

SHIRLEY. I bet it was.

MORT. A wonderful dream. We carried on like we did in the Poconos. Remember the Poconos? Hm?

SHIRLEY. Do I remember the Poconos! *(They laugh. He embraces her. They kiss. Shirley finds it strangely unsatisfying; Mort is oblivious to her depression.)*

MORT. Oh, Shirley ... I thought I was never gonna hold you like this again. You know what that was like?

SHIRLEY. I know. *(She breaks the embrace and resumes puttering; Mort follows her around the room.)*

MORT. Let's go to bed.

SHIRLEY. What? *(Mort cocks his head toward the bedroom.)* You gotta be kidding.

MORT. No. Why?

SHIRLEY. Just like that? In the middle of the day? You're an animal.

MORT. I *am* an animal. *(He nuzzles her neck.)*

SHIRLEY. *(Good-naturedly evades him.)* Down, Morty.

MORT. What, you're worried about him? *(Meaning Artie.)* We'll shut our door. He'll get the message.

SHIRLEY. No, no, it's not that. I can't sleep with you, Morty.

MORT. Who's talking about sleep?

SHIRLEY. I mean, I don't feel sexy anymore. Isn't that funny? Me?! I don't feel sexy.

MORT. You'll lie down, it'll come back to you. That's all I ask: Let me look at you sideways again.

SHIRLEY. No, no, Morty trust me. It wouldn't be the same.

MORT. It's like riding a bike, like swimming. Put down the rag, stop with the dusting.

SHIRLEY. No! What have I just been saying?! Things are different now, Morty. I can't anymore. All that's over, too.

MORT. Don't say that!

SHIRLEY. It is, it's over I said! *(She eludes him as Mort playfully chases her around the room.)*

MORT. Oh, I get it ... You want to play, hm?

SHIRLEY. No ...

MORT. Okay we'll play ...

SHIRLEY. Come on, stop ...

MORT. I'm gonna get you!

SHIRLEY. No, Morty ... please ...

MORT. I'm gonna get you, Shirley!

SHIRLEY. *(Calls.)* Artie? Artie?

MORT. What are you calling *him* for?

ARTIE. *(Off.)* What.

MORT. Shirley please, I want us to go to bed.

SHIRLEY. *(Calls.)* Tell me how your date went!

38

MORT. What?! What date?

SHIRLEY. *(To Mort.)* Remember he had a date? You know: Pam. *(Calls.)* How'd it go last week you and Pam?

ARTIE. *(Off.)* Fine.

MORT. You don't want me anymore? Is that it?

SHIRLEY. Morty, stop, I didn't say that.

MORT. We'll talk. Come on. We'll go inside, lie down and talk. Okay? We'll take it slow. We'll see what happens.

SHIRLEY. *(Shakes her head, takes his hand comfortingly. A beat. Calls.)* Artie, come here a minute.

MORT. *(Annoyed.)* Wonderful. Call Artie. *(Artie stands near the entrance to the kitchen.)*

ARTIE. What.

SHIRLEY. You had a nice time?

ARTIE. I had a nice time.

SHIRLEY. She came over?

ARTIE. She came over. Okay? *(Returns to the kitchen.)*

MORT. This is the *girl* you're talking about? The college girl?

SHIRLEY. Yeah. *(Calls.)* Do anything special?

ARTIE. *(Returns.)* What are all these questions?!

SHIRLEY. Nothing. I just want to know did you stay in, did you go out to eat?

ARTIE. We stayed in.

SHIRLEY. Good. That's all I wanted to know. *(Artie goes. She calls.)* Artie?

ARTIE. *(Off.)* What!

SHIRLEY. Did anything ... happen?

ARTIE. *(At the entrance.)* What do you mean?

SHIRLEY. *You* know.

ARTIE. *(Returns to kitchen, blushing.)* Ma-a ...

SHIRLEY. Uh-oh, I'll take that as a yes.

MORT. *(Embarrassed but proud.)* You mean him and that girl?

SHIRLEY. Uh-huh. *(Calls.)* Congratulations! *(Artie groans in the kitchen.)* Say something to him.

MORT. Yeah? Like what?

SHIRLEY. I don't know, something ... fatherly. You've got to try talking to him, Morty.

MORT. I'm no good at that.

SHIRLEY. Try.

MORT. *(Calls.)* Artie?

ARTIE. *(Off, annoyed.)* What?

MORT. C'mere a minute. *(A beat. Artie enters with coffee; Mort beams at him.)* So! How do you like that! *(Playfully roughs up Artie.)* Son of a gun. He looks different to me already. Doesn't he? Big shot, you don't say a word, hm? You don't say a word to your dad? *(More roughhousing and hair mussing, which Artie enjoys.)*

SHIRLEY. *(During the above.)* Well, good. I had a feeling.

ARTIE. You did? What do you mean?

SHIRLEY. You seemed ripe to me. Ready. I thought it would be nice if we got out of your way and let you have the place to yourself.

MORT. See what a mother you have?

SHIRLEY. Seemed like the perfect night to shlep your father out to eat. *(A beat.)*

MORT. Wait, when was this?

SHIRLEY. Last week.

ARTIE. *(A beat.)* Oh, God ...

MORT. Wait a minute ... This is the night we went out for Chinks you're talking about?

ARTIE. Oh, no ...

SHIRLEY. Uh-huh.

ARTIE. This is too much ...

MORT. Shirley, what are you saying?!

ARTIE. I don't believe this ...

SHIRLEY. I wanted to try that new restaurant. You know how I love grand openings.

MORT. You made me go out to eat so he could get laid?!

SHIRLEY. Shhh ...

ARTIE. You died for my sins, Ma.

SHIRLEY. Don't be a jerk.

MORT. You mean to tell me your mother is eating her last supper and you're up here screwing some girl?!

ARTIE. She's not "some" girl!

SHIRLEY. Morty ...

MORT. That's what was going on here?!

SHIRLEY. Don't make it worse.

ARTIE. *(To Shirley.)* I wanted you out of the house but I didn't mean permanently!

SHIRLEY. Of course you didn't.

MORT. Look how you stick up for him!

ARTIE. I knew it was all my fault! I knew it! I knew it!

SHIRLEY. Artie, stop it! It's nobody's fault! It happened! You had nothing to do with it!

MORT. You're always on his side, no matter what! He comes first! Ever since he was born!

SHIRLEY. Morty, the kid hurts. Help him!

MORT. I lost you 'cause of him, Shirley, don't you see that?! It's 'cause of him we went out to eat in the first place! I wanted to go to the deli! But no! You had to try this new Chinese restaurant!

SHIRLEY. Morty ...

MORT. I always gave in to you! Whatever you wanted! If only I put my foot down this one time! This one time! If only I insisted! But, no! No! And look what happened! *(Starts to exit to the bedroom.)*

SHIRLEY. Where are you going?

MORT. I got a headache. I want to lie down.

SHIRLEY. Morty, don't go, I need you with the furniture ...

MORT. I want to lie down, I said! *(Mort exits. Pause.)*

SHIRLEY. Oh, boy ... *(A beat.)* Don't do this to yourself. Come on. Stop beating yourself up. I gave you a gift, Artie. A present. *(A beat.)* Was it good at least? *(Artie shrugs equivocally.)* It gets better, believe me.

ARTIE. He's had it in for me for years.

SHIRLEY. No, he hasn't.

ARTIE. I always felt like a foreign exchange student around here and you were my interpreter. Without you, our words just kinda bump up against each other and make noise. Ma, you don't know what it's like here without you.

SHIRLEY. Sweetheart ...

ARTIE. How could you do that to me?! How could you leave me alone with him?!

SHIRLEY. He's your father, he loves you!

ARTIE. He doesn't know me. We have nothing to say to each other! *(A beat.)* Did he make you happy?

SHIRLEY. What?! What kind of question is that? Of course he made me happy. He's a very sweet man, your father. We were very

41

happy.
ARTIE. You were?
SHIRLEY. Oh, yeah. We really had something.
ARTIE. What?
SHIRLEY. Something special.
ARTIE. What, what made it special?
SHIRLEY. I don't know. I can't put it in words.
ARTIE. Try.
SHIRLEY. Artie ...
ARTIE. I need to know.
SHIRLEY. *(A beat.)* It's little things.
ARTIE. Like what?
SHIRLEY. It's ... the way people felt about us. People envied us. Friends. Are you kidding? Friends were jealous of our marriage, that's how special we were. Everybody's favorite couple, that was us.
ARTIE. Then why were you so restless all the time?
SHIRLEY. Restless? I wasn't restless.
ARTIE. Yeah, you were. You were always changing things. You were never satisfied.
SHIRLEY. I was a perfectionist.
ARTIE. You always had this thing about the furniture. Once I came home from school at three o'clock and the living room was completely rearranged. I thought I went into the wrong apartment by mistake.
SHIRLEY. That's not 'cause I was restless. That's 'cause I was always coming up with new ideas.
ARTIE. Why wouldn't you just leave things the way they were if you were really happy with them?
SHIRLEY. I don't know ...
ARTIE. You used to change your hair color like practically every week.
SHIRLEY. Not every week. I was experimenting with tints.
ARTIE. It was very confusing when I was little. I never knew what you'd show up looking like in my dreams.
SHIRLEY. So big deal. So I dyed my hair. I liked trying new things. What's wrong with that?
ARTIE. *(A beat.)* Ma, I know about the Holiday Inn.
SHIRLEY. What Holiday Inn?

ARTIE. The Holiday Inn in Freehold, New Jersey.

SHIRLEY. I don't know what you're talking about.

ARTIE. It's okay. Daddy doesn't know.

SHIRLEY. *(A beat.)* Artie, your imagination is going wild. *(They took at one another for a beat.)* You wouldn't understand.

ARTIE. Oh, but I do. I'm saying it's okay, Ma. I understand. You were restless.

SHIRLEY. Why do you keep using that word?

ARTIE. Well, you're here, aren't you? *(A beat. The front door opens and Sid pokes his head in.)*

SID. Hell-o-o ...

ARTIE. Oh, shit ... Hi, Pop!

SHIRLEY. Sidney!

ARTIE. *(To Shirley.)* I forgot to tell you ...

SID. Ceil dropped me off. She's circling. No place to park. Bella went to pick up an Entenmann's. I gotta pee. *(He heads for the kitchen; Artie grabs him and steers him in the right direction.)* By the way, Shirley, I was very sorry to hear what happened. *(He exits into the bathroom.)*

SHIRLEY. Oh, God, company's coming, I can't have the house looking like this ... Give me a hand ... *(They arrange furniture. Sid enters from the bathroom. He follows them from place to place, which contributes to his confusion.)*

SID. False alarm. My prostate. Don't have the reservoir I had in my youth. Once I could hold my water hundreds of miles at a time.

SHIRLEY. How are you, Sidney?

SID. How am I? Doctor says I'm a medical miracle. Should've been dead by now. Getting another cataract, this time in my *left* eye, 'cause I liked the one in my *right* eye so much. I blink and I blink but the picture don't get sharp. *(Squinting at her.)* How are *you*, by the way?

SHIRLEY. I'm fine, Sidney.

SID. "Sidney." Always "Sidney." Never "Pop," never "Sid." "Sidney." *(Whispers.)* Artie, she was away, right? What was it? A milk farm or something?

ARTIE. Well, no, Pop, she ...

SID. *(Without waiting for a response.)* Nice to see you, Shirley.

SHIRLEY. Thanks, Sidney, it's nice to see *you*.

SID. What was I gonna do? Stay home? Never should've retired. Used to have a pinochle game? Now I have solitaire. Bella hates cards. All I need is to break my hip. Kiss of death. One day my mother's making gefilte fish from scratch, the day after that ... My mother passed away, I was fifty-seven years old and I cried like a baby. *(To Artie.)* Where was she? In the hospital?

ARTIE. No, not the hospital, Pop.

SID. Careful, don't pop any stitches. You look good, Shirley.

SHIRLEY. You think so?

SID. We should throw a party for you now that you're back. How about that anniversary party you and Morty threw for us?

SHIRLEY. You still remember that party?

SID. Like it was this minute.

ARTIE. What party?

SID. Before you were born. Before my diabetes, before Ceil got divorced, before Bella's hysterectomy ... *(To Shirley.)* Everybody was still alive. My sister Ruth was alive, *you* were alive. My mother. My mother passed away ...

SHIRLEY. So you liked that party, hm, Sidney?

SID. What a party! How come we don't have parties anymore? Anybody left to invite? Everybody's gone or going. *I'm* going, *you're* gone. Was it a surprise party?

SHIRLEY. Sure.

SID. Yeah? Were we surprised?

SHIRLEY. I think so, or at least you pretended to be.

SID. I remember the cake: everything from Ebinger's. Blackout cakes.

SHIRLEY. That's right.

SID. Streamers ... balloons sticking to the walls ... *(To Artie.)* How is it they stick to the walls?

ARTIE. Static electricity.

SID. Is that what it is? Amazing. It was like New Year's Eve. And all our friends. How'd you get hold of all our friends?

SHIRLEY. Phone calls.

SID. Wasn't that some party? Who was there?

SHIRLEY. All your friends.

SID. Artie, it was one of those once-in-a-lifetime times, everybody you ever knew right there in one house! Then, everybody went home! A messy house, crushed pretzels in the carpet. Bella was on her hands and knees picking up crumbs and you didn't even mind 'cause there were so many nice things to talk about while you did the dishes. And I bet she doesn't remember, but she danced with me.

ARTIE. Yeah?

SHIRLEY. I did?

SID. See? I knew it: She doesn't remember.

SHIRLEY. I danced with a lot of people.

SID. *(To Artie.)* You ever dance with her?

ARTIE. I don't think so.

SHIRLEY. You don't think so? I tried to get you to dance with me at your bar mitzvah. You put up such a stink. *(To Sid.)* Big shot. Too old to dance with his mother.

SID. His loss. *(To Artie.)* She was some dancer. *(Becoming more urgent.)* We danced together, you and me. Bunny Berigan was on the hi-fi. I held you close! You threw your head back and laughed. Your hair was auburn then. Red lipstick smudged on your teeth. Shirley, Shirley, Shirley ... I held you close! You wore a burgundy dress with a sash. *(To Artie.)* Oh, God, she doesn't remember.

SHIRLEY. Sidney, you're gonna get yourself sick.

SID. I held you so close, Shirley. You threw your head back and laughed.

ARTIE. Pop, calm down ...

SID. She laughed! She could've slapped my face but she didn't! *(To Shirley.)* Why didn't you slap my face?

SHIRLEY. What are you talking about, Sidney? Why would I slap you?

SID. *(Reaching for her.)* Come here ...

SHIRLEY. Why?

SID. I want to show you. *(He tries to take Shirley's hands but she pulls away.)* What's the matter?

SHIRLEY. My hands are cold.

SID. *(Taking her hands.)* Don't be ridiculous. They're like toast. *(Humming Vernon Duke and Ira Gershwin's "I Can't Get Started,"* he dances with her; she laughs.)* I'm crazy about that laugh of yours.

* See Special Note on Songs and Recordings on copyright page.

45

Look at those eyelashes. Look at that mouth. Oy, Morty doesn't know what he's got.

SHIRLEY. He knows.

SID. If he knows what he's got, he doesn't know what to *do* with it now that he's got it.

SHIRLEY. Sidney!

SID. "Sidney!" *(They dance slowly for a while.)*

SHIRLEY. *(Suddenly.)* Sidney! You were making a pass at me! *(They stop dancing.)*

SID. *(Distressed.)* Of course I was! What did you think I was doing?

SHIRLEY. In front of all those people?

SID. Nobody saw. Maybe Morty did. Yeah, I think maybe Morty gave me a look.

SHIRLEY. Sidney ... I didn't know ...

SID. *(A beat.)* You mean ... all these years ... I was ashamed of something you didn't even know I did? I kept quiet. I kept my distance. I took naps. I thought you thought I was a monster.

SHIRLEY. No, I just thought you were tired.

SID. No ... Shirley ... it was that little dance we had, you and me, that dance, at that party, with the streamers and the balloons on the walls, and that laugh of yours with your head thrown back so gorgeously ... *(She slips back into Sid's arms and they dance slowly around the room, Artie watching them. Sid sings the last phrase of "I Can't Get Started."* To Artie.)* Didn't I tell you she was some dancer? *(Doorbell. Shirley goes to answer the door.)*

ARTIE. Wait! Let me get it. Hide.

SHIRLEY. Why?

ARTIE. Please? Get in there till I tell you to come out. This has got to be timed just right.

SHIRLEY. Artie, you're a weird kid.

ARTIE. I know. *(Shirley goes into the bathroom; Artie shuts the door. Doorbell.)* Do me a favor, Pop, don't tell them she's here.

SID. You mean it'll be like a surprise party?

ARTIE. Yeah, a surprise party.

SID. Oh, good ... *(Goes to the door.)* Just a second ... *(Fumbles*

---

* See Special Note on Songs and Recordings on copyright page.

with the locks.)
ARTIE. Pop ... Pop, I'll do it. *(Artie unlocks the door. Bella, holding a grocery bag with an Entenmann's cake in it, enters, followed by Ceil; they're in the middle of a conversation.)*
BELLA. So he was a little overweight.
SID. Hell-o-o ...
BELLA. Hello, Artie, darling. *(She kisses Artie.)*
ARTIE. Hi.
CEIL. He was fat! Hiya, Artie. *(She gives Artie her cheek to kiss.)*
ARTIE. Hiya.
BELLA. Maybe if you showed him a little love, he'd sign up with Weight Watchers.
CEIL. Ma-a ... *(Takes the bag from Bella, starts for the kitchen.)*
ARTIE. Notice anything different?
BELLA. I was just saying to myself ... Look what's going on here, Ceil.
CEIL. I see! *(Exits.)*
SID. So? How's everything?
BELLA. *(Looking around.)* What is it, Sid.
SID. Nothing. I just wanted to know how's everything.
BELLA. Everything is fine. Your daughter let another one get away, otherwise everything is fine. Artie, darling, you're arranging?
ARTIE. That's what it looks like.
BELLA. All by yourself?
ARTIE. Well ...
SID. Shhh ...
ARTIE. I had a little help.
BELLA. You mean your father?!
CEIL. *(Returns; excitedly.)* Remember the stove last night, Ma, how disgusting? *(Takes Bella's hand, leads her to the kitchen.)* Get ready for the shock of your life. My kitchen should only look like this. *(They're gone.)*
SID. *(To Artie.)* If we had even a couple balloons ...
BELLA. *(Off.)* Oh, my God!
SID. ... a red and a pink ...
CEIL. *(Off.)* Is that spotless or is that spotless?
SID. ... Rub 'em against the wall...! *(Shirley, holding Comet and a sponge, pokes her head in from the bathroom.)*

47

SHIRLEY. How long am I supposed to stay in here?

ARTIE. Not yet! Get back!

SHIRLEY. All right, I'll do the tub. *(As Artie shuts Shirley in the bathroom, Bella returns, followed by Ceil holding a cake.)*

BELLA. *(Enters kvelling.)* I knew I'd get through to them. *(Seeing the bathroom door close, she goes to it.)* Is that my Morty? Hm?

ARTIE. Uh, Grandma...?

BELLA. I was up the whole night worrying.

CEIL. *(Noshing on cake.)* I know.

BELLA. *(At the bathroom door.)* Morty? Momma is so proud of what you accomplished, sweetheart. Hurry so I can eat you up. *(Mort enters from the bedroom; Bella is somewhat confused. Artie is enjoying this.)* Oh, *there* you are.

MORT. *(Beaming.)* Did you see?

BELLA. I certainly did.

MORT. Is that something?

BELLA. It's marvelous.

MORT. Who would believe such a thing, right?

BELLA. Not me.

MORT. Never in a million years.

BELLA. Never. Give Momma a smooch. *(They embrace.)* Mazel tov, Morty. That kitchen, it's a work of art.

MORT. Tell that to the artist. Where is she? *(Artie gestures to the bathroom. Mort nods. A beat.)*

BELLA. Mort? Is there a cleaning girl in your bathroom?

MORT. What are you talking about, Ma? I asked if you saw her.

BELLA. Who?

MORT. Shirley!

SID. *(Silencing Mort.)* Shhh ...

BELLA. What do you mean Shirley?

CEIL. Oh, God, Ma ...

BELLA. Shirley came all the way over to clean the house?

MORT. *(Laughs.)* Yes! Artie, tell them.

SID. *(To Artie.)* Where was she anyway?

CEIL. What's gonna be with Morty?

MORT. *(Prodding Artie.)* Tell them.

ARTIE. *(Matter-of-factly.)* It's true. She came home.

SID. Shhh ... supposed to be a surprise ...

CEIL. Artie ...

BELLA. *(To Artie.)* Enough with the jokes!

CEIL. Why torture him?

ARTIE. She's home! My mother came home!

BELLA. Comedian!

MORT. No, she did! She rang the door! You should've seen her standing there, my poor baby, she walked all the way ...

CEIL. You're breaking my heart, Mort.

BELLA. Look what you're doing to your sister.

MORT. The two of us, I'm telling you, we were beside ourselves. Right, Artie? *(He and Artie share a laugh.)*

CEIL. Oh, God ... *(Exits to bedroom.)*

BELLA. *(Takes Mort's hand.)* Listen to me: Grief, Mort ...

MORT. *(Smiling.)* Ma ...

BELLA. It does things to people.

ARTIE. *(Enjoying the fuss.)* She's in the bathroom, Grandma.

BELLA. When will you stop? When we have to put him away?

ARTIE. See for yourself. Open the door! She's scrubbing the bathtub!

BELLA. A little respect for the dead, Artie. *(Ceil enters, donning Shirley's fur jacket.)*

MORT. Oh no you don't ...

BELLA. Good, Ceil.

MORT. Put it back!

CEIL. It's for your own good, Morty ...

MORT. You can't just go to her closet and take things!

BELLA. Ceil is right! You gotta snap out of it, Morty!

MORT. Shirley's not gonna like this ...

CEIL. Shirley doesn't need it anymore, she's dead, Mort ...

SID. *(To himself.)* Is that what I heard? Dead?

CEIL. *(To Mort, continued.)* Dead and buried. I'm alive, let me enjoy it.

BELLA. That's right.

CEIL. Shirley would've wanted it this way.

MORT. *(Calls.)* Shirley! *(Bella shakes her head sadly at Mort's display.)*

CEIL. *(Models for Sid's approval.)* Daddy?

MORT. *(Calls.)* Ceil's got on your beautiful jacket!

CEIL. What do you think, Daddy, hm?

49

SID. Nice.

MORT. *(Now struggling with Ceil.)* All right, take it off! Take it off!

CEIL. Morty, stop! She's dead, Morty! Shirley is dead! You gotta let go! *(Artie opens the bathroom door, revealing Shirley.)*

ARTIE. Tadahhh!

SHIRLEY. Hi.

MORT. There's my Shirley!

SID. SURPRISE!

SHIRLEY. There was a ring around that bathtub you would not believe. Sit down, break in a chair! What can I get you? *(Bella and Ceil are stunned into silence.)*

BELLA. *(Her eyes on Shirley.)* Ceil, my glasses are in my bag. *(Ceil hands it to her.)* Thank you, dear. *(Finds her glasses, puts them on, looks at Shirley for a beat.)* Does that look like Shirley to you, Ceil?

MORT. It's Shirley.

BELLA. I'm asking Ceil. Ceil?

CEIL. Yeah, Ma.

BELLA. *(A beat.)* So, Shirley? *(A beat.)* Good for you.

MORT. See? What did I tell you? She was here all along!

SHIRLEY. *(To Bella.)* What do you think of the place? It's getting there, don't you think? I'm finally getting it right. Please. Don't mind me. Everybody sit.

CEIL. *(Taking off the jacket.)* Shirley ... I didn't mean anything ...

SHIRLEY. That's okay, Ceil.

CEIL. I only wanted to see how it felt.

SHIRLEY. That fur ... always made me feel like a million bucks.

CEIL. You always had such nice things, such pretty things.

SHIRLEY. Thanks, Ceil. You always *kibitzed* with the men at cousin's club meetings; I helped in the kitchen. You always made the men laugh. Follow the sound of men laughing: There was Shirley. You always looked good. Everybody thought so. My father ... *(Strokes the jacket lining.)* I always loved that: "Shirley" stitched inside in fancy script. *(She puts down the jacket.)*

BELLA. *(To Mort.)* So did you find out about your shirts at least?

MORT. Oh, yeah, Shirley, what'd you do with the laundry ticket for all my shirts?

BELLA. He's out of clean shirts.

SHIRLEY. Oh! *(Goes to the front closet, takes a paper-wrapped*

Chinese laundry bundle from a shelf.) They were right here! I never got a chance to put them away!

MORT. Ha! How do you like that!

BELLA. *(Unenthused.)* Leave it to Shirley to solve the big mystery.

SHIRLEY. What's the matter, Bella, aren't you glad to see me?

BELLA. Glad? Glad is not the word. *(She walks away from Shirley.)*

MORT. Ma, what's the matter with you? Is that how you talk to Shirley? After all she's been through?

BELLA. What do you want me to say? "Welcome home, Shirley"? I can't. I don't approve.

SHIRLEY. You? You never approved.

BELLA. I beg your pardon? I approved more than you know. More than you know, young lady. I'm not the kind of person who shows much. I'm not like your father-in-law in that respect.

SID. Huh?

BELLA. Nothing, Sid. *(Continuing, to Shirley.)* This I don't approve. I saw you laid out in the chapel, Shirley. I watched them close the lid and put you in the ground and cover you up with dirt.

MORT. Ma, why even bring that up?

BELLA. Why?! 'Cause the dead don't dust, my darling! The dead don't redecorate!

MORT. Ma, what do you want to make waves for?

BELLA. This isn't right, Morty! This is not how it's supposed to be. *(To Shirley, gently.)* Look: You're in the middle of supper, the middle of redecorating, the middle of your life: It happens. Too bad about you. You don't get to keep a foot in the door. You're either in or you're out. And you, my dear Shirley, you are not in.

MORT. What kind of way is that to talk?! I'm not gonna have you talk to my wife like that!

BELLA. *(To Shirley.)* You think this is helping him? You think this is helping either of them?

MORT. Never mind about me. I have a tongue. I can speak for myself.

BELLA. *(To Shirley.)* And just how long do you expect to keep this up?

SHIRLEY. As long as the boys need me, I'll be here.

BELLA. Is that so? And that's okay with you, Artie?

51

ARTIE. What?

BELLA. It's okay with you having your dead mother around like this? *(Artie doesn't know what to say.)*

MORT. All right, that's it. If you don't approve ... go! Goodbye!

SHIRLEY. Morty ...

MORT. Leave us alone!

BELLA. Fine! Let's leave them alone with dead Shirley. Ceil? Sid? *(Gets her coat, etc.)*

SHIRLEY. Don't go, we're family!

CEIL. *(Waking Sid.)* Stop dreaming, Pop, we're going home.

SID. *(Waking from a dream; being helped into his coat.)* Shirley?

SHIRLEY. Come on, sit down, eat your cake. We'll talk.

MORT. *(To Shirley.)* Forget about them. All they want is to keep you buried. We don't need them.

ARTIE. We don't?

MORT. We don't need anybody. The hell with them.

BELLA. You know, Shirley? Quite a number of people came to pay respects.

SHIRLEY. Yes?

BELLA. Many many people came to the chapel.

SHIRLEY. Really?

BELLA. Oh, the place was jammed. And here, people in and out all week. Neighbors, old friends from the Year One ... The food they sent! The platters! So many donations, so many trees planted!

CEIL. *(Anxious to leave.)* Ma-a ...

BELLA. I'm coming. *(To Shirley.)* I guess what I'm getting at, Shirley ... What do we tell all these people? They went to all that trouble. *(A beat. As she touches Mort's face in a gesture of farewell.)* You know my number. Artie? You've got your whole life. Time heals. *(Artie kisses her cheek. A beat.)* Shirley, you should rest in peace. *(Bella exits. Ceil, holding Sid, starts for the door.)*

CEIL. By the way, Shirley, in case you were wondering ... That was me ... I was the one wrapped up all the leftovers.

SHIRLEY. Thank you, Ceil, I appreciate it. You did a wonderful job.

CEIL. You think so?

SHIRLEY. Ceil? *(She offers the jacket. A beat.)* Take it. It's yours.

CEIL. I couldn't ...

SHIRLEY. Please. I want you to have it. *(She puts it in Ceil's hands.)* Wear it in good health. *(A beat. Sid approaches Shirley.)*

SID. Shirley? *(Ceil tugs on Sid's arm. To Ceil.)* Let go my arm.

CEIL. Say goodbye, Pop.

SID. Let go my arm. Shirley? *(To Ceil.)* Don't pull on me!

CEIL. Oh, the hell with it! *(She exits.)*

SID. Shirley? When I'm sleeping? Driving home? *You're* the one sitting next to me, Shirley, *you* are, the road map on your lap, reading me directions. *(He kisses Shirley's forehead.)* See you soon. *(He starts to exit.)*

ARTIE. *(Goes to hug him.)* Bye, Pop. *(Sid pats Artie on the cheek and exits.)*

MORT. *(To Artie.)* Lock the door. *(Artie's anxiety is growing; he doesn't lock the door.)*

SHIRLEY. But, Morty, they're your family.

MORT. This is my family right here.

ARTIE. Dad ...

MORT. It's like a dream come true! We're together again, Shirley! Nothing else matters.

SHIRLEY. I don't know about this, Morty ...

MORT. All I want is to be with you. Artie and I'll keep you company. Right, Artie? Artie, lock the door.

ARTIE. Why?

MORT. We don't want anybody from out there coming in.

ARTIE. Dad, you don't mean it ...

MORT. Just do it. *(To Shirley, as they sit down together.)* Are we gonna have ourselves a ball! It'll be like a vacation, only we'll stay home.

SHIRLEY. But you're gonna have to go back to work.

MORT. The hell with work.

SHIRLEY. You're gonna have to earn a living. You've got Artie to take care of.

MORT. Why bother to leave the house when I can stay here and be with you?

SHIRLEY. I don't want you doing that for me, Morty.

MORT. Nothing out there is important anymore, Shirley. We don't have to go anywhere, we don't have to see anybody, we don't have to do a thing. Nothing would make me happier than just sitting here knowing you're next to me. *(He rests his head on her shoulder. Shirley's discomfort is growing.)* Artie, I told you to lock the door.

ARTIE. No.

MORT. What do you mean no? Do you love your mother or what?

ARTIE. Of course.

MORT. Then lock the door.

ARTIE. If I lock everybody out, that means I'm locking us in. I don't want to lock us in. Mommy, Grandma was right, this isn't gonna work. You shouldn't be here anymore.

MORT. Hey! If you don't like it, you can go, too!

SHIRLEY. Morty, don't say that.

MORT. He wants to get rid of you, Shirley!

ARTIE. No, I don't!

MORT. Yes you do! That's what you're doing! You want to push your mother out that door forever? Is that what you want?!

ARTIE. No! I don't *want* her to go! *(To Shirley.)* You're tricking me again! I saw you rise away on a wave! But you're really gone this time! You can't come back.

SHIRLEY. But I haven't finished taking care of you!

MORT. Don't listen to him, don't listen to him, Shirley ...

ARTIE. How am I gonna miss you if you won't go?!

MORT. *(Pushing Artie around.)* Everything's always you! What about me this time?!

ARTIE. Daddy, you think I want this?

SHIRLEY. *(Overlap.)* Morty, stop it ... Leave him alone!

MORT. *(To Artie.)* If you don't want her around, then you should go!

SHIRLEY. But *I'm* the one who's dead!

MORT. No, no ... not for me you're not. You're not dead. You'll never be dead. Shirley, I'll do anything you want ...

SHIRLEY. Morty ...

MORT. I'll make it easy for you here. What do you want? Tell me.

SHIRLEY. Morty, stop this ...

MORT. You don't have to lift a finger. Tell me what to do! *(He holds Shirley to him and carries her around the room.)* YOU CAN'T GO!

SHIRLEY. *(Struggling.)* Mort!

54

MORT. I'm nothing without you!

SHIRLEY. Artie, help me!

ARTIE. *(Trying to separate them.)* Dad ...

MORT. I could hold on to you like this forever!

SHIRLEY. *(Overlap.)* No, Morty ... stop!

ARTIE. *(Furiously trying to pry them apart.)* Daddy, stop! I don't want to lose you, too! *(Pause. Mort slowly releases her. A beat.)*

MORT. *(To Artie, gently.)* Me? I'm here. *(Pause.)*

SHIRLEY. Such a stupid death.

ARTIE. I know.

SHIRLEY. Not what I had in mind at all. Killed by a piece of pork stuck in my windpipe?! Is that stupid?!

ARTIE. It really is.

MORT. So it went down the wrong pipe. So what? Could've happened to anybody.

SHIRLEY. Oh, but those poor people who run the restaurant! It was their grand opening! And all those hungry people waiting in line?! I must've ruined their appetites!

MORT. *(Comforting her.)* Shhh ...

SHIRLEY. One minute I'm tasting plum sauce, the next thing I know, I'm on the floor, drowning.

ARTIE. Did you see your whole life passing...?

SHIRLEY. No, just feet. Feet of Chinese waiters. *(A beat.)* I never felt so cheated in my life.

ARTIE. I'm sorry, Ma.

SHIRLEY. Why couldn't I have gone slowly? Hm, Morty? Like in the movies. Could've had bedside scenes. Long good-byes. Me, in pink lacy nightgowns, and perfume. We could've prepared together. I could've tidied up, nice and neat. Wouldn't I have been great, Artie? Cheerful, cynical ...

ARTIE. *(Smiling.)* Yeah ...

SHIRLEY. ... valiant till the end, withering away with dignity?

MORT. Shirley, all that matters is you're here and you're staying here.

SHIRLEY. *(To Artie.)* I can't stay, can I? *(Artie shakes his head. A beat. Shirley begins to make finishing touches. Pause.)*

MORT. Look ... Maybe we can work something out.

SHIRLEY. I don't think so.

MORT. Maybe you can stay a little while longer.

SHIRLEY. No, Morty, I can't.

MORT. A couple more days, even.

ARTIE. Dad, no.

MORT. You can spend weekends here or something.

SHIRLEY. No, Morty, I don't think that would work.

MORT. No? *(She shakes her head. A beat.)* What'll I do, Shirley?

SHIRLEY. You'll learn new things.

MORT. I can't.

SHIRLEY. You'll have to.

MORT. It's too late.

SHIRLEY. Of course it's not, Morty, don't be ridiculous. *(Pause.)*

MORT. You're really going, Shirley?

SHIRLEY. Yes.

MORT. When? Soon?

SHIRLEY. A couple of minutes.

MORT. That soon, hm? *(Her eyes on Artie, Shirley nods. Pause.)* I just want you to know I'm not crazy about this.

SHIRLEY. I'm not either, really.

MORT. You can still change your mind.

SHIRLEY. No. *(Pause.)*

MORT. You're always welcome here. Remember that.

SHIRLEY. I know.

MORT. I mean it.

SHIRLEY. I know, Morty, thank you. *(Pause.)*

MORT. So … How you getting back?

SHIRLEY. Same way I got here.

MORT. Oh, no you're not. I'm taking you.

SHIRLEY. You really don't have to.

MORT. You think I'm gonna let you go off by yourself? I'll drop you off.

SHIRLEY. Yeah?

MORT. How's that?

SHIRLEY. That sounds nice.

MORT. I'm just gonna have to stop for gas. Tell you what: Why don't we make a little trip out of it? I'll drive slow. We'll take our time.

SHIRLEY. Okay.

MORT. We'll take in the scenery.

SHIRLEY. Nice.

MORT. And if you get hungry, I'll take you to that seafood place. Remember how you loved their bay scallops?

SHIRLEY. Mmmm ... yes...!

MORT. And if we pass any flea markets along the road?, we'll stop, I won't say a word.

SHIRLEY. Thanks.

MORT. No big deal.

SHIRLEY. Good.

MORT. No rush.

SHIRLEY. No rush. *(A beat.)* I'm gonna go put on something pretty.

MORT. Good idea.

SHIRLEY. I'll be right back. *(She exits to the bedroom.)*

MORT. *(Calls.)* Take your time! *(A long, awkward pause, like in Act One when Mort and Artie are alone for the first time.)* Artie?

ARTIE. Yeah? *(A beat.)*

MORT. I'm not mad at you.

ARTIE. Oh?

MORT. You're not mad at *me* are ya?

ARTIE. Mad? Not mad. *(A beat.)*

MORT. So I guess this is just one of those things, huh?

ARTIE. I guess. *(A beat.)*

MORT. Gee, I sure wish this didn't have to be.

ARTIE. Me, too. *(A beat.)*

MORT. Must be rough losing your mother. I mean, I wouldn't know what that's like. *(Artie looks at him. A beat.)* You know I think you're a good kid, don'tcha, Artie?

ARTIE. Yeah?

MORT. Always thought so. *(A beat.)* Hey, I don't suppose you'd maybe want to go away with me to Hawaii or someplace, would you?

ARTIE. No, Dad.

MORT. No, hm? Didn't think so. Not such a good idea, hm? *(Artie shakes his head no.)* No, I guess not. *(A beat.)* Who knows? Maybe I'll go by myself. How does that grab ya?

ARTIE. Yeah, you should.

MORT. I will. I'll get a tan, I'll eat pineapple. I'll send you postcards. How's that? Can I send you postcards?

ARTIE. Of course.

MORT. *(Suddenly near tears.)* I don't know what I'm gonna do, Artie ... You gotta help me.

ARTIE. Daddy, I can't. *(Pause. Mort nods. A beat; he sees that Artie's shoelace is untied and ties it for him.)*

MORT. Careful. You could hurt yourself. *(Shirley enters wearing the red dress.)* Oh! Would you get a load of this!

SHIRLEY. You like it?

MORT. Fabulous!

SHIRLEY. It's not too loud?

MORT. If it is, the hell with them. You look beautiful. Artie, doesn't your mother look beautiful?

ARTIE. Yeah, she really does.

MORT. *(To Shirley.)* Let's see you shimmer. *(Shirley shakes.)* Look at that!

ARTIE. Could you go now? Please?

MORT. Uh, yeah, sure ... *(To Shirley.)* You want to take anything with you?

SHIRLEY. Like what? *(Artie takes the matchbook out of his pocket and looks at it.)*

MORT. I don't know some pictures, maybe? Pictures of us? *(He looks through the drawer of the sideboard for photos. Artie hands her the matchbook. She looks at it quizzically, then it registers.)*

SHIRLEY. "Holiday Inn, Freehold —" *(She and Artie look at one another. She puts the matchbook in her purse as Mort hands her some photos.)* No, I don't need pictures. I'll remember. *(She admires the room.)* Well!

ARTIE. Nice. *(Shirley is tempted to rearrange a pillow; Artie gently stops her.)* Just leave it. It looks good.

SHIRLEY. Yeah? What do you think, Morty? Not bad, hm?

MORT. What are you talking about "Not bad"? *Good.*

SHIRLEY. *(A beat.)* "Goodbyee forevverr ... " *(Nervous laugh.)*

ARTIE. *(Quietly.)* Please ... just go?

SHIRLEY. Say goodbye? *(Artie looks at her after for a moment, then turns away. A beat. She smiles.)* Okay.

MORT. Artie, will I see you later? *(Artie shrugs, "I guess.")* How about when I come back, I take you out to eat? Hm?

ARTIE. Sure. *(Shirley and Mort start to exit; she stops to admire the room.)*

SHIRLEY. Isn't it amazing what a little rearranging'll do? *(A beat. She exits; Mort follows her out, then sticks his head in.)*

MORT. Artie? Lock up. *(Mort closes the door. Artie, alone, is confronted by the silence and his own grief. He walks around the room for a moment, then suddenly goes to the front door, opens it, and calls down the hall.)*

ARTIE. Mommy?! *(A beat. He slowly shuts the door. As the lights fade, he looks like he is finally about to cry.)*

PROPERTY LIST

Polaroid snapshot (MORT, ARTIE)
Bagels (ARTIE)
Tissue (ARTIE)
Orange (ARTIE)
Hardened gob of gum (ARTIE)
Matchbook (ARTIE)
Glass of water (ARTIE)
Magazine (BELLA)
Plum (SID)
Foil, to wrap food (ARTIE)
Tupperware container (CEIL)
Medicine bottle containing pills (BELLA)
Coats (ARTIE)
Women's clothing on hangers, red sequined dress (BELLA)
Box of cards (CEIL)
Address book (CEIL)
Thank-you note (ARTIE)
Tray of food and utensils (ARTIE):
    Bagels
    2 cans of Tab
    Cream cheese container
Towel (SHIRLEY)
Jam jar (MORT)
Dying flowers (SHIRLEY)
Vacuum cleaner (SHIRLEY)
Sweater (ARTIE)
Cup of coffee (ARTIE)
Grocery bag (BELLA)
Comet and sponge (SHIRLEY)
Entenmann's cake (CEIL)
Eyeglasses (BELLA)
Fur jacket (CEIL)
Paper-wrapped laundry bundle (SHIRLEY)

SOUND EFFECTS

Doorbell
Running shower

NEW PLAYS

★ **SHEL'S SHORTS by Shel Silverstein.** Lauded poet, songwriter and author of children's books, the incomparable Shel Silverstein's short plays are deeply infused with the same wicked sense of humor that made him famous. "...[a] childlike honesty and twisted sense of humor." *–Boston Herald.* "...terse dialogue and an absurdity laced with a tang of dread give [*Shel's Shorts*] more than a trace of Samuel Beckett's comic existentialism." *–Boston Phoenix.* [flexible casting] ISBN: 0-8222-1897-6

★ **AN ADULT EVENING OF SHEL SILVERSTEIN by Shel Silverstein.** Welcome to the darkly comic world of Shel Silverstein, a world where nothing is as it seems and where the most innocent conversation can turn menacing in an instant. These ten most imaginative plays vary widely in content, but the style is unmistakable. "...[*An Adult Evening*] shows off Silverstein's virtuosic gift for wordplay...[and] sends the audience out...with a clear appreciation of human nature as perverse and laughable." *–NY Times.* [flexible casting] ISBN: 0-8222-1873-9

★ **WHERE'S MY MONEY? by John Patrick Shanley.** A caustic and sardonic vivisection of the institution of marriage, laced with the author's inimitable razor-sharp wit. "...Shanley's gift for acid-laced one-liners and emotionally tumescent exchanges is certainly potent..." *–Variety.* "...lively, smart, occasionally scary and rich in reverse wisdom." *–NY Times.* [3M, 3W] ISBN: 0-8222-1865-8

★ **A FEW STOUT INDIVIDUALS by John Guare.** A wonderfully screwy comedy-drama that figures Ulysses S. Grant in the throes of writing his memoirs, surrounded by a cast of fantastical characters, including the Emperor and Empress of Japan, the opera star Adelina Patti and Mark Twain. "Guare's smarts, passion and creativity skyrocket to awesome heights..." *–Star Ledger.* "...precisely the kind of good new play that you might call an everyday miracle...every minute of it is fresh and newly alive..." *–Village Voice.* [10M, 3W] ISBN: 0-8222-1907-7

★ **BREATH, BOOM by Kia Corthron.** A look at fourteen years in the life of Prix, a Bronx native, from her ruthless girl-gang leadership at sixteen through her coming to maturity at thirty. "...vivid world, believable and eye-opening, a place worthy of a dramatic visit, where no one would want to live but many have to." *–NY Times.* "...rich with humor, terse vernacular strength and gritty detail..." *–Variety.* [1M, 9W] ISBN: 0-8222-1849-6

★ **THE LATE HENRY MOSS by Sam Shepard.** Two antagonistic brothers, Ray and Earl, are brought together after their father, Henry Moss, is found dead in his seedy New Mexico home in this classic Shepard tale. "...His singular gift has been for building mysteries out of the ordinary ingredients of American family life..." *–NY Times.* "...rich moments ...Shepard finds gold." *–LA Times.* [7M, 1W] ISBN: 0-8222-1858-5

★ **THE CARPETBAGGER'S CHILDREN by Horton Foote.** One family's history spanning from the Civil War to WWII is recounted by three sisters in evocative, intertwining monologues. "...bittersweet music—[a] rhapsody of ambivalence...in its modest, garrulous way...theatrically daring." *–The New Yorker.* [3W] ISBN: 0-8222-1843-7

★ **THE NINA VARIATIONS by Steven Dietz.** In this funny, fierce and heartbreaking homage to *The Seagull*, Dietz puts Chekhov's star-crossed lovers in a room and doesn't let them out. "A perfect little jewel of a play..." *–Shepherdstown Chronicle.* "...a delightful revelation of a writer at play; and also an odd, haunting, moving theater piece of lingering beauty." *–Eastside Journal (Seattle).* [1M, 1W (flexible casting)] ISBN: 0-8222-1891-7

DRAMATISTS PLAY SERVICE, INC.
440 Park Avenue South, New York, NY 10016 212-683-8960 Fax 212-213-1539
postmaster@dramatists.com   www.dramatists.com